Become a Youtuber

Tactics and Tricks to Boost Your Video Ranking on Youtube

(Make Money Off of Youtube& Tips Tricks and Secrets for Youtube Success)

Cary Coleman

Published By **Jordan Levy**

Cary Coleman

Become a Youtuber: Tactics and Tricks to Boost Your Video Ranking on Youtube (Make Money Off of Youtube& Tips Tricks and Secrets for Youtube Success)

ISBN 978-1-998901-54-8

Legal & Disclaimer

Table Of Contents

Chapter 1: How To Make Money On YouTube

YouTube is making it easier to become a celebrity. You don't need to be supported by an established media company to rise to fame and earn a lot of money by the process. But as you realize, simple doesn't always mean easy. This is the same for being an YouTube Star - it's simple but it's very difficult.

Why am I saying it's easy? It's because the basic business model or method of earning money is quite simple. It's also known as...

Advertisements

The most popular and most popular method many people earn money through YouTube. It is the primary and first business model, too. How does this advertising thing work? Two ways that this can be done in direct advertising as well as product placements. Let's examine Direct advertising for the first.

In essence, direct advertising on YouTube is the same as what you watch on TV. Companies pay for their commercials on YouTube. The difference is in the way businesses pay for these advertisements. There are two ways that companies pay for commercials or ads they show on YouTube cost per visit (CPC) as well as cost per 1,000 views (CPM).

If companies choose to advertise through CPC They only pay for ads that people do click. This means that if the viewer doesn't actually click on an advertisement, the company isn't liable for that specific instance. Therefore, if you find that the CPC for a specific phrase is set at $2 then the advertiser is charged $2 for the click. If there were 1000 clicks on the particular advertisement and the advertiser is be charged $2,000! Clickable advertisements are displayed in the lower portion of the display screen when the video is playing or as a rectangular banner that appears on the right of the channel that that video is playing.

If companies choose to use CPM that is to pay for ads by calculating viewer impressions. This is defined as when viewers watch their ads for more than 30 seconds. In essence, it's an advertisement that relies on sustained watching. Even if a person clicks on the advertisement several times, but doesn't stay on the screen for longer thirty seconds or more, the company advertising will not be financially liable.

What's in it to the viewers, Sparky? The first is that you will not earn any money from advertisers unless the viewers click the ads displayed while they view your videos, or unless viewers view it for more than 30 minutes. Do not think that when you pay CPC and CPM for an advertisement's $2.00 for $10 or $2.00, for instance, all the money is yours. Nope...you'll only get a tiny fraction of it since YouTube is the sole owner of the platform and demands more of the revenue pie to pay all of the costs involved in maintaining the platform. It's completely unfair to hop onto their site, upload your videos and receive all the money you want, right?

It was really easy was it? I said it! Did I not say that it's not always simple? Yeah, I did.

What is the reason you might ask? First, think about this: to make an impressive amount of money through YouTube there are two things: a huge audience and sufficient engagement. Let's look more closely at the audience first.

It's no surprise that when advertisers pay for each impression or click they make on the ads they place on your videos there is a good chance that the higher the amount of people who see the videos you've uploaded, the more the revenue from advertising you'll earn. But getting lots of people to see your videos - also known as audience building, something we'll talk about in greater in depth - isn't easy. Given that you're competing with million of similar videos YouTube it is necessary to put in the effort and work cleverly to build your following and gain enough crucial mass to generate an income of a substantial amount from YouTube. It's good to know that it's not rocket science, and If you follow the tips I'll provide in the next chapter, the chances of building your following will be significantly increased.

Let's look at engagement, and no it's not about getting married yet! Although your video's viewership or numbers of viewers are the basis for making thousands of dollars through YouTube however, it's not the only factor that will result in plenty of cash for you. What matters is the interaction of your viewers or their engagement with the ads in your videos. Naturally, there won't be any engagement if there are no viewers, but even if your video had been seen by millions of people however, none of them viewers clicked on ads or watched for long enough time to surpass the 30-second minimum however, you'll still get $0.00! This is why your efforts should not be confined to viewers but must continue to engage the viewers.

More than saying "How much views will my video require for me to earn hundreds of thousands?", you should also be asking "How many views are my videos required to get?"

Have Attention, Make Money

Since engagement, not just viewing is the most important factor in making the most money on

YouTube and other platforms, you'll need to develop strategies that are sound to attract the attention of of the appropriate type of viewers. Think about it this way: when you have create your YouTube channel properly and upload the correct types of content, you'll be able to draw the right advertisers and the correct viewers who are likely to watch or click on advertisements that you have posted on your channel. You can accomplish this by:

* Concentrating: If you wish to get quality advertisers, you must to make sure that your channel is not scattered! Don't make your channel a jack-of-all-trades-master-of-none type by uploading videos on basketball, makeup, and cooking! Advertisers like channels that cater to particular demographics which are ideal for their product since it offers their ads better chances of earning customers.

In the beginning prior to putting together or record your very first YouTube video you need to make sure that the YouTube channel you create is a highly targeted one. We'll talk about how to identify the most profitable market to your channel on YouTube that will give you the needed attention.

The Key is It's In the Words (words) A aspect you should be aware of is that your CPC can vary depending on the keywords you choose to use in your videos. You can determine which keywords perform better by examination of the CPC that is typically determined through a bidding process which you as a content creator do not have to worry about. What you must be aware of about is CPCs for terms that relate to your channel or videos.

* Let's use two terms "debt repayments" in addition to "cheap guitars" as examples of theoretical reasoning. Let's say that debt payments have an CPC of $10.00 as opposed to $3.00 for low-cost guitars. This means that in the general scheme of things, marketers believe that using "debt repayments" as a keyword, instead of "cheap guitars" will provide them with the highest yield in terms of the actual number of clicks for the same number of views. "Cheap guitars" might have a view count of 1,000,000 , but if just 3 people actually click

advertisements for these keywords, advertisers would rather to use a keyword that has only 50,000 views and thousand people using ads.

What's that has to do with you? It's best to use keywords with a high CPC to maximize your potential YouTube revenue. Not only will you earn more money per click, but also more clicks.

* Create Your Video Production Schedule in the best way one of the factors that will assist you in building your fan base and build your brand on is consistency in frequency of uploading content as well as the quality of your content. It is recommended to adopt a factory or assembly line method which is where the video production so to shoot a single video at each period, shoot a number of videos at each time. This helps you save time and effort, and allows you to regularly produce videos that viewers might come to expect.

* You may be able to come out with a wildly popular video, but if you do not follow it up with a new high-quality video, you'll run the chance of losing your viewers' attention. By the

time you've created with fresh material, it's gone. Additionally, having only the one or two video uploaded to your channel per year can cause your channel to become a boring and boring one. So ensure that you organize your video production schedule carefully to regularly produce quality content that will not only catch the eye, but stay in it.

Product Placements

Apart from direct advertising, another method you could earn income through your YouTube channel includes product endorsements. This is whenever an advertisement or sponsor gives you - the creator and the owner of the channel or video an amount in exchange for a direct critique of their goods or services in your channel or videos, or for including or mentioning them in the.

The more popular the number of viewers your videos greater, the more valuable they are to advertisers or sponsors. So, your odds of making even more money from your channel are more likely. This is why, for products, your most important focus is on viewership or the

the number of views. There's no need to engage here, Sparky!

Because the number of people who watch is crucial for direct advertising as well as products, so we'll take on the issue of how to grow your YouTube viewers to a critical mass in a future chapter.

Other Ways To Make Money From YouTube

One of my favourite TV channels would say...but wait , there's more! Making money with YouTube isn't restricted to the two primary models of business I mentioned earlier.

The common wisdom goes like that: upload your videos to the internet, people view them, and you earn money. This is the premise that some online marketing hucksters sell to a lot of unsuspecting customers to convince them to buy their"get rich quick" strategies. While you can earn an income from being a YouTube content producer or creator however, only a small percentage of individuals are capable of doing this. Most times the best scenario is that users can utilize YouTube as a alternative source of income rather than as a primary source.

The reason is that you're not able to benefit from the entire amount of money advertisers pay YouTube to advertise direct, like I mentioned earlier. You'll likely get in the range of 5-10% from CPC or CPC also known as CPM. For instance, if you're CPM for a particular phrase that you use within your post is around $20, then you'll receive between $1 and $2 of that. Think about it this way - should you wish to earn more than $1,000 a month from your YouTube content through CPM that's about 1 million to 500,000 views per month, which could be a huge amount for any YouTube channel owner.

The positive side lies in the fact that you have more than two ways to get the most from this cat known as YouTube. Here are some additional ways to earn income from YouTube videos.

Sell On YouTube

Who said only businesses could market their services on YouTube? You too can! If you have a business that you operate and especially an online-based one You can start YouTube channels for the promotion of your company. It's true: YouTube is actually the largest search engine in the world, and it's not even named Google! If you're able produce good videos that are based on the right keywords, you could sell a lot of your items through this social media platform.

If you already have products or services to market, you could make videos that are targeted to your market's niche and add links to the description section so that they can be directed to your company's primary site or landing pages.

Affiliate Links

In addition to selling your own goods or services, you are also able to offer other people's or businesses products and services using affiliate marketing. You'll be provided with a specific affiliate link that you can insert into the descriptions of your videos. The links will lead users to website that the company is selling. Affiliate links are unique to you, which allows the seller to identify the websites of their users - and ultimately buyers were referred to them by you. They can then know that you were accountable for these sales and pay you commissions on those sales.

Get Gigs

YouTube can be used by YouTube to establish your self as a thought-leader or a respected resource for specific topics to attract people to request speaking engagements or other events. For instance, you could make your own YouTube channel which is geared towards helping people to get their financial affairs in order. When you fill your channel with excellent videos about personal finance, which offer practical solutions to viewers' financial concerns, your fame and recognition will rise until people will ask you to hold seminars and workshops, which will be paid, naturally!

An inspiring illustration of this are The Piano Guys, a group of 4 fathers from Utah that became so well-known on YouTube they could receive gigs on a regular basis and were contracted by the world's largest company, Sony. The channel was set up mostly to advertise their store which was appropriately named - guess that right the Piano Guys! One of them even claimed that they had already earned millions through YouTube however they had not sold a single piano!

It doesn't matter if you're a performer, a speaker or an expert in all things make-up and beauty, you can utilize YouTube to showcase your work and earn a high-paying gig.

Chapter 2: The Setup

Once you've figured out the various ways to earn money from YouTube now is the time to get in the right direction and start your own business! Let's start with the most basicoption, which is to start an account on YouTube even if you don't own one already.

Creating Your Channel

It's a good thing that the process of setting up the YouTube Channel is the most straightforward thing to do inside this manual. It only takes about a minute of your time. After you've finished creating your channel, you can modify it using some of the options available so that your channel is distinctive and distinct. This can includes, among other things, uploading your image or company's logo, as well as linking your business or personal Facebook and Twitter accounts with your YouTube channel.

The first step is to sign-up to get a free Google account. You might be wondering "Ain't I creating a YouTube channel , but it's not an email address? What's the deal? ...?" Do I do? Relax Sparky is that YouTube is controlled by Google and you'll require an email address associated with an YouTube account much in exactly the same way that your Facebook account as well as other online accounts require the use of an email account. And the best part about this is that the Google account grants access to numerous options which includes YouTube.

Okay, enough with the tinkering. I strongly recommend the creation of a separate account or a separate Google/YouTube account for your business or income-generating reasons so that you can keep your private life private. Be aware that you'll have to reach a certain level of celebrity status if are looking to earn a substantial amount of money via YouTube and if you're using an account for your own personal, it's time to say goodbye to the private space. Another advantage of having an account that is different in comparison to your personal account is that you are able to give other people the responsibility to run your YouTube channel in the event that you become too well-known or busy to manage it.

Let's get into the essentials of creating the Google account: Google account:

If you are using a computer's internet browser start typing www.youtube.com within the menu bar.

When you're on the homepage of YouTube you can click on the box that reads "Sign In" It's located in the upper-right corner of the page.

* If the "Sign in" screen appears click on the link that reads "Create an Account" This will appear on the upper-right corner on the page. After that, you'll be able to create a brand new Google account. Remember - I've informed you

that you'd be creating an account on Google account!

* If the screen that reads "Create Your New Google Account" appears then fill in the fields in the detail section that will contain your initial as well as your last name(s). After you've completed identifying yourself, you'll be asked to choose your own unique username for Google. Then, you'll have to establish and verify that your brand-new Google account's password. You'll also be asked to provide additional crucial details like the date of birth, gender, email address, as well as mobile phone number.

* As previously mentioned don't make use of your personal account for this, if you want to keep your privacy. Therefore, do not make use of your email address address as your email address when you are asked to enter it.

Once you have identified your location via the drop-down menu, you must agree to Google's terms of service which will appear by the screen before clicking on the button which states "Next step" to continue.

Be aware that the Google user name you select is your YouTube channel's user name , so make sure you choose it carefully! Remember that first impressions are the most important and the first impression you make will be your username. If you are planning to launch a personal finance channel that needs to be branded with a professional appearance, names like "CrabberCrazy" as well as "DungeonDude" is an absolute turn-off! Find something that is appealing that is memorable, catchy and in the end, simple to remember. What's the benefit of a cool name that people are able to forget, right? Additionally, you will receive an unpaid Gmail address to use with YouTube. YouTube account.

* You'll then need to create your own Google Account Profile, which includes a profile picture

(uploading's an option). If you're planning to upload a photo for your profile just click "Add the Profile Picture" and you're good go. If you're creating an official profile for your company you should think about using your company's logo or business product for your profile picture. After that, simply click "Next Next Step" to continue the process of creating an account. When you're finished you'll be able to return to YouTube by clicking "Back to YouTube".

* You'll then receive two emails: one to confirm your current email address, and the second with the information for your brand new Gmail account and you need to save for later reference. For verification emails you need to click on the link provided to verify your email address. Your account is verified within a few minutes.

Once you have your Google account running It's time to start creating your personal YouTube channel which you'll start your videos to earn money! This is the last step before you shoot your first video, which could be the catalyst to propel you to fame as well as a little money.

You can visit YouTube. * Go to the YouTube webpage and log up using your brand-new Google account username and password. After you've signed in you'll be taken to the main page of YouTube.

Take a look at the upper right-hand corner in the upper-right corner of your homescreen, and you'll see your profile photo. To open the menu for accounts on Google you need to click on your profile photo. The drop-down menu will show up within the same space and, when it appears you click on "My Channel".

* Once you open the "Create Your YouTube channel"" screen shows up, you'll see many items, including your profile picture the user's

name, username, as well as your first and last name. Click "Edit" that is connected by the button "From Your Google Profile" to modify you Google account's preferences. The profile you create is what visitors or people who visit your profile view on the internet.

Just below the heading, which reads "Activities you'll share on Your Channel" There are choices labeled Like A Movie Comment on a Video, Share A Favorite Video, and Subscribe to A Channel. Select the options for activities that you'd like your viewers to have access to whenever they go to your channel. Once you're done, click "OK Now I'm Ready to Continue" to complete the creation of your YouTube channel.

If you weren't keen on making money through YouTube The next step is to start creating videos and then populating your channel that you've just created with videos. However, since you're looking to make money from the videos you've made you'll need to take an additional step to be taken that is to make money from your brand new channel.

Chapter 3: Show Me The Money

Making money from your YouTube channel does not require an PhD or a Master's degree in any field. It's that easy that I'll be able to explain the process in this section! This is the final step to set up your account that you'll have to finish before heading off to filming editing, uploading, and submitting your videos to your channel.

But before we talk about this, we need to talk about something first.

How Monetization Works On YouTube

As we mentioned in Chapter 1 YouTube places ads in or near to the videos viewers watch on their site. YouTube doesn't assume that you'll like it and put advertisements on your videos or close to them. You'll first need to turn on the monetization option for your account (which is easy) and then send a request for approval for monetization to for each video. Additionally, you'll need have two other accounts that can be connected with your YouTube account to be eligible for the advertising earnings the videos earn that you earn. You'll need an AdSense account as well as an account with PayPal one.

You can get an AdSense account through Google at no cost. Be sure to be at minimum 18 years old, since if you're not, you'll require an adult help get started. After you've created the AdSense accounts, you'll have to connect it with an PayPal account. AdSense will transfer the revenue from advertising you made through YouTube. In addition, through PayPal you can access your funds through the payment of the credit card bill via your bank account at the local branch.

The most important factor or prerequisite for your videos to be monetized is the absolute ownership of worldwide commercial rights to everything that is in them. When I refer to everything, I'm talking about the music and video footages or songs that you use in your videos have to be your own original creations or you have the legal authority from the copyright owner. If you include songs whose copyrights you don't have or copyrighted footage the video will not be monetized. If you'd like more information about this issue, simply visit the YouTube Copyright Center. In addition the videos you upload for monetization are required to be compliant to YouTube's terms of Service and Community Guidelines.

Monetizing Your Channel

To make money from the value of your YouTube videos, just select the tab that monetizes your videos "Monetize with Ads" box. It is displayed when you upload your videos. If, for any reason, you've forgotten to monetize an uploaded video, just visit Video Manager and click on the "$" icon that appears next to the video you didn't make monetization.

While it might be logical to earn money from your videos once they are uploaded, it could be better in terms of financials to make money from each video after it has been seen by a substantial number of viewers already. Why? The chance is high that your first-time viewers might be shut off immediately after viewing advertisements. Keep in mind that, beyond numerous views, you'll want to create an audience of regularly-visitors or customers. This increases the chances of increasing the number of subscribers, and decreases the risk of denying them in the first. If your channel has a steady flow of subscribers or viewers, you're already monetizing uploaded videos. Then, you can begin to monetize new videos as you upload.

Don't expect to become one millionaire in a matter of minutes on YouTube. Don't think of making a thousand dollars in a matter of minutes. The key is in having a huge audience with a high level of engagement. The process of acquiring both isn't easy in the event that you're not already famous in the first place. Be patient, because there are times when good things happen to those who persevere and keep striving for the goal of success.

Monitor Your Stats

Uploading your videos isn't the only part of the story. In order to create an audience with high levels of engagement you'll have to learn the best practices for your content and what doesn't. The only way to determine that is by analyzing how your video and channel by analyzing the available data.

It's easy to accomplish this. Click on your channel's menu and select Analytics, which will allow you to access your videos and channel's Video Views as well as demographics of these views. If you've already utilized monetization for your channel and your videos the option allows you to see estimated earnings and the performance of your ads. This information will help you determine how your videos are doing well or not (number of viewers) and what categories of people react more strongly to your channel and video (Demographics). It is also possible to do an analysis of historical data to see if your strategies are effective or not (increasing numbers of subscribers and viewers as well as changes to estimates of earnings and performance for every month). The more you know about the numbers, the better you can improve or modify your current video content strategies to ensure that your videos are performing better and enable you to realize your dreams of making hundreds of dollars from your videos.

Another great source of feedback that can help you make sure you're staying on the right path in regards to the videos you're uploading to your channel is the viewer's feedback, which you will find in the comments area of the videos you upload as well as the number of shares and likes. These are indications of how your viewers feel about your channel and the videos, therefore, the more positive comments, likes , and shares more favorable it is for you. If you don't have a lot or none, this could suggest that your content isn't creating a strong emotional impression on viewers, which suggests that you should review your strategies for video content.

Chapter 4: Producing Viral-Worthy Videos

The primary factor that determines whether you'll be able to build a large enough number of subscribers with a sufficient amount of engagement is the content, i.e. the videos you upload. That's the primary reason people will keep returning to your channel to watch more. In simple terms, you cannot be able to afford uploading videos which are "Ok" or "Good" You'll have create videos that look amazing and that make people say "Wow" and "Awesome!". It is essential to create videos that people would be compelled to discuss and then share.

That is you'll need to make viral videos.

Viral-Worthy Characteristics

While viral videos are often unplanned or "accidental" however, that doesn't mean that you can't take steps to increase your chances of getting viral or becoming at the very least, virally-worthy. It's possible to plan your videos carefully to make sure it meets at least one, if not more of the following features:

Quick And Great

It's important to keep in mind the fact that this is a time and age in which the majority of people are on the internet and everyone - even you - must deal with the issue of information overflow. The most common way that people handle a flood of information is to make rapid judgments about the quality of any information or information they see. Have you ever wondered why Twitter is popular despite the fact that it has a character limit of just 140 characters?

The majority of users who visit the internet and watch YouTube videos aren't able to find the time to sit and watch lots of videos. As such they'd rather watch videos that catch their attention from the start and provide valuable information or entertainment in an hour or less. You can see that many of the shorter videos on YouTube with under 10 minutes have significantly more views or views than those with lengthy lengths i.e. over 15 minutes long, with the only exception is the ones that have already become famous in the first place.

Another factor to take into consideration is a study conducted in the form of The New York Times. The study discovered that 19% of viewers quit watching videos within 10 seconds. Nearly half the viewers - 44%, to be precise were done within the first minute. If you don't have enough reason to keep things fast and enjoyable I'm not sure what else.

It's not enough to be quick and good however. You'll have to be careful even with the relatively short length. Being aware that you'll lose around 50% of your video's viewers in the first few minutes it is essential to arrange your videos in that the most intriguing, hilarious fascinating and intriguing details are placed at the top. Particularly, you should place them in the initial 60 second of your videos. In the event that you don't, your video could be afflicted by a high rate of death and will be not worthy of being shared on the internet. This is a case in which the old adage "save the top for the end" isn't just a bad idea, but could be fatal.

Cheerio

It's not about breakfast snacks. I'm talking about the overall impression or mood that your content. They must be generally positive or positive if they be able to go viral, or at the very least being virally worthy.

In his best-selling book "Contagious What Happens When Things Catch On" the author Jonah Berger explains that the most popular posts are ones that trigger strong emotions in readers or viewers and the most shareable of which are positive or upbeat. Berger and a co-researcher Katherine Milkman Katherine Milkman - discovered that in terms of sharing capabilities (or the possibility of going viral, should I claim that's the case) positive emotions usually outnumber negative emotions.

The point? Create videos that are upbeat or positive, if you'd like to increase the chance of being popular.

Relevant

Your videos might be short and awesome, and just as energetic as Mary Poppins but if they're about what happened in the Watergate Scandal, then by all means, it's not as viral like Richard Simmons' aerobics videos (I feel something burning in my lungs and it's probably the fats in your body!). Your videos need to be relevant to current events in order to get substantial traction with a large number of people. In other words, how many people are interested in watching the videos and sharing them on social media to the point of virality or value?

One method to make your videos more relevant is to use current trends or popular memes or subjects. Making use of this method will increase the likelihood of your video becoming popular and winning new subscribers and increase engagement levels.

It's recommended to increase your knowledge of pop culture for excellent ideas for video content. For instance, the Piano Guys, whom I've previously mentioned, get the majority of their ideas for current pop songs to incorporate into the videos they make from their teenagers. Their children have also been helping their dads extremely well and you can see the amount of money these guys have earned from YouTube in addition to how they've secured the biggest recording contract for one of the most prestigious label companies in the world, Sony Music.

More Than Entertain, Engage

The most important thing that the majority or all YouTube videos that go viral is engagement. It gives you the possibility of not having to be a one-hit sensation, but to become a regular success. Without it, you'll not be able to attract the attention and respect from your viewers, which means that your videos will not be viewed as viral. Keep in mind that the majority of people love the feeling of being involved, e.g., be and heard by others or being asked their thoughts. The Old Spice brand was able to capitalize on this fundamental human trait.

One of the commercial campaign in one of their advertising campaigns, the actor who was playing the role of the Old Spice actor answered questions asked by followers on social media in a series of quick and simple YouTube videos. Through answering questions on videos, Old Spice engaged many people, and also gained more fans and followers through giving them the chance to ask questions which were answered by YouTube. Asking questions to viewers and then responding obviously in public, as well as conducting contests are among the most effective ways to interact with viewers and gain the trust of more faithful and engaged viewers for your videos. This helps your videos become viral.

Impart New Knowledge

Another method to increase the virality of your video is to impart new information to your audience. They're always eager to find out something new, whether it's an individual productivity tip or simply some new and exciting information about famous companies or people. When your viewers feel that they've got the inside scoop about the amazing details in your videos They'll want to share it immediately so they can claim the privilege of claiming it in their friends. When more of their friends agree and more of your videos are likely to go viral.

Inspire

Relevant content is always valuable and relevant, particularly when it's about things that people in general experience or relate to, regardless of what's trending or not. For example, financial issues all year out, no matter who's President or Oscar recipient for Best Actor and Actress, most people face problems with finances and, as an outcome, a well-produced video on overcoming financial difficulties has the potential of being viral.

So if that at some point, you're not getting any relevant and useful concepts for the next video think about releasing extremely inspiring ideas that fall within your channel's specialization.

How To Plan Your Quality Videos

No one - not even you has ever thought of failing in the course of their work, however, failing to plan is equivalent to planning to fail. Before you even set out to pack your equipment and begin recording, you should make sure you plan your videos carefully to ensure that you're able to produce high-quality videos with the least amount of time and effort.

If the primary goal of the videos you create is for them to make them viral or get the attention of most people The first thing you'll have to take into consideration is the topic and subtopics. If your content isn't appealing, you'll be leaving behind an army of faithful users. However, even if your subject isn't appealing making a plan ahead can give you the chance to figure out how to present your topic in a way that makes fascinating.

When you are planning your video's content, it can help you to follow the method that non-fiction writers take: creating an outline. Many of these writers come up with a subject, and then break it into smaller pieces or sub-topics. This way you will have a clear understanding of the flow of your video to be logical to viewers. If you convey ideas or facts in your videos with an orderly and rational manner viewers will enjoy your videos, and they may send them to their acquaintances. And the more viral your videos get and the more popular they are, the more likely you'll be able to earn substantial money on YouTube.

Another aspect to be aware of when planning your video is to consider the long term, i.e., not only one video at a given time however, several videos at one time. This will make each of your videos more effective in terms of consistency and giving a bigger image. If you are planning each video in a single sequence it's possible that the shift or change in subject matter or conversation between the videos on your channel could be abrupt, which isn't nice in any way. Imagine watching a video about the process of getting debt free this week? This is followed by another video about investing in the following week which is followed by another personal debts related video in the third week?

Another advantage of planning multiple videos simultaneously is that it lets you increase interest or excitement. If you are planning a series of videos that are part of a series, you provide your viewers only enough information to satisfy their hunger and inspire them to return. You won't be able to achieve that by preparing just one or two videos at an time.

You must also think about planning the proper terms for the videos you upload. It's very difficult to get the right amount of traffic to your YouTube revenue-generating goals if don't include the appropriate keywords in your video's description and tag. In order to do this, you'll need to become familiar with Google's keyword tool to be aware of which keywords are most popular, and which you can include in the description of your videos in the future.

Apart from determining what keywords you can use for your videos, it is important to be working to improve your transcription. They serve two crucial reasons. If you're not the spontaneity kind of person and require some substantial speaking on footage, having a written transcript will allow you to say what you're supposed to say on camera which will reduce the amount of times you take per video or for each segment.

Another reason to use the transcript, and in particular post-recording transcripts, where you write down the content of the video immediately after you have shot it in order to upload it to YouTube through the description part of the video. In this way, you increase the likelihood for major search engines such as Google making it appear higher on their results pages for specific terms.

Chapter 5: Producing High Quality Videos For Your Channel

After discussing the key features of viral videos It's time to discuss the technical aspects of how to create high-quality video content for YouTube. YouTube Channel. However current, pertinent, fast and simple, inspirational interesting, informative, or informative it is, the truth is that a badly shot or made video has the same chance of winning like a turtle winning the 100-meter race in a tournament for amateurs. It is important to speak about some of the fundamental technical aspects to shooting high-quality videos to ensure that your videos can be watched at a high quality, attention-grabbing, and focus-grabbing to get the attention of and captivate the attention of many viewers. This increases your chances of making money from YouTube through direct advertisements and product placement channels.

Go Easy On The Zoom

One of the most frequent errors that creators of video content on YouTube make is to use excessive zoom. This could make your videos appear like a toddler , or even more likely, it can cause your viewers' heads turn. If you must zoom out or in be sure to make it happen in a gradual, steady method. If you have to make a sudden zoom, don't do it immediately . Allow enough time to be allowed for users to adapt.

When it comes to zoom, another factor that can impact what you can expect from your footage is how much digital zoom is used instead of optical zoom. Zooming optically isn't always as effective in the sense that you can see more of an object from a distance, however you're not at risk of having your video pixelated. Utilizing the digital zoom of your camera can result in videos with appear pixelated, which does not bode well for the quality of their content.

Framing

A lot of people like shooting photos or videos with subjects that are directly on the center. This isn't the most effective method of presenting your subject. While it's not illegal to do this, or harm the visual, it's not the ideal method to present your subject. Since your goal is to make high-quality videos that can be viewed by the masses and entertaining, good doesn't suffice. You must create a well-structured video.

What's the most effective way to achieve this? Fill the frame of your video with your subject. Don't place them close to the center and use a small amount of center focus. It adds more character or the life of your videos if the subject is a slightly off to either the left or right. It's not my fault, but it's just what it is.

Don't Always Go Wide

In addition to shooting scenes designed at capturing the scene It's not a good option to choose large shots that allow you to observe a lot, but not enough details. The focus of a woman waiting to catch the bus will certainly be a more appealing video clip rather than one with a large number of passengers waiting to catch the bus in the street.

Multi-Angled Shots

Even if your video or scenes aren't spectacular in way and are shot from only one perspective or angle could make a fascinating video that is as exciting like a speed-drag racing event. Did you notice how dialog scenes in films or television shows frequently shift perspectives or angles dependent on the character speaking? This is because a single angle is sure to cause viewers to be bored to death. Do yourself and your viewers an favor by using various angles when making videos to avoid boredom death.

Not Against The Light

If you're shooting footage of your subject, ensure that you - as the cameraperson isn't looking or pointing against the lighting. Why? It could cause backlighting, which can greatly dim the perspective on the camera.

It's easy to think that since we can observe the finer details of faces, even when the light is emanating from behind (or in front of us) that cameras are able to record the same detail. In most cases, backlighting results in a subject with a dark appearance but with very minimal or no detail being surrounded by a halo illumination. It is best to shift your location so that you're not directly the vicinity of the source of light.

Use Three Legs

One of the most unpleasant things that could occur to a flawlessly shot video is that it shakes. It's difficult for the eyes to see a film that shakes or vibrates continuously. A tripod can ensure that this won't occur.

Although many modern cameras and even video editing software have stabilization options but nothing can beat the actual thing. Consider these functions as pirated renditions the stability your videos get when you use the tripod. There's no reason to not use one since the majority of good tripods are available at a reasonable price.

Chapter 6: Building Your Audience

While it's true that high-quality videos that are virally able are essential for attracting many viewers, it's not always enough to increase your reach. When we speak about creating your following, we're not only talking about a large number of viewers. We're talking about a lot of regular and high-quality users, i.e., highly attracted. To achieve this you need to think beyond just individual videos. You'll have to think about the bigger and bigger. In this article we'll look at ways to create a strong audience through big image thinking and acting.

Find Your Niche First...

When the term "niche" is employed in the business world it means focusing on a specific market part of the larger broad one. In order to be capable of making a substantial profit through YouTube niche refers to a particular topic which your videos revolve around. Examples of this include investment, Paleo cooking, and bodybuilding. By focusing on a certain subject, you'll be in a position to attract regular readers because they'll be able to anticipate that you'll be able to provide new content which they're attracted to or passionate about.

While it's tempting to make an all-encompassing channel in which your attention is solely on you and the things you're interested in, unfortunately the odds of such a channel's success are as high as the size of a molecule. Today's viewers want distinctive content that is centered around a specific subject or issue. It's therefore ideal to identify your niche before you start your channel on YouTube. Here are some helpful suggestions for locating the right topic to your channel on YouTube.

Go Sub

Choose the general subject first, before selecting a subtopic within that general subject. For example, you choose to do a sports channel. If you stop at this level, it is too general or wide to be able to garner enough attention among sports enthusiasts, which is why you'll have to find another sub-topic. This could be football, basketball or baseball. By focusing on a particular sport in this case you'll be able to offer lots of interesting content and details to viewers who are passionate about a specific sport and you'll have the chance to create loyal followers or viewers who are likely to check out every video and give you the level of engagement for your channel and the videos. This is because they know what they can be expecting from you channel. Also, remember that it's not just only views, engagement and they're regular ones too.

Your Channel In A Sentence

It will be easy to determine if your topic is precise or specific enough when you can define the content of your YouTube channel in a single sentence. If you're not able to do that clearly define your channel, it's an sign that your channel isn't sufficient in terms of specificity and that it's not sufficiently broad. In this scenario, you'll need think about your niche anew.

Being specific enough with regards to your area of expertise makes it easy for viewers to anticipate the type of content you'll often produce for your YouTube channel. If they're satisfied with the first impressions they get the expectations they have will help you to execute your YouTube advertising efforts well. Make your one-sentence descriptions appealing and easy to remember , so that people will keep your YouTube channel on the forefront of their mind whenever they think of the subject or topic of their choice.

Unique Selling Proposition (USP)

The ideal segment to target for your YouTube channel would be one in which your channel or the videos you make can be unique and stand out. If you can find one in which there's only one person with the ability to provide this type of video content, you're essentially an exclusive market and you've got an entire market! The more distinctive you are in your field and the more people wish to join your channel since it's only through you that they'll have the ability to view specific types of video content that pertain to the subject of a particular niche or.

...Then Build Your Audience...

Once you've decided on a category or topic to focus your creativity on, you're ready to start working and create your channel's following. If I've not stressed it enough, a active and engaged audience will increase your potential to become viral that will result in a number of dividends to you when it comes to product placement and advertising profits through your YouTube channel. Here are some practical methods to do it.

It's All About The Content

As I've mentioned before and a few times I'll add that the most important ingredient in your YouTube financial success is high-quality content. It's what allows you to gain faithful and highly engaged fans or subscribers. These are the primary keys to the realm of YouTube cash! The significance of this is apparent from the fact I've dedicated two chapters to making quality video content.

Consistency And Routine

Viewers or users won't be enticed or interested enough to become your regular audience, i.e., subscribers in the event that they don't get regular access to your top-quality videos. This is why it's essential to establish your content schedule for video at least a month ahead. This means that you determine when you'll be releasing new videos during the month or week , and according to that frequency, you decide on the number of videos you'll need to upload, and at what times during the week. The anticipation is an excellent way to keep your viewers interested in your channel. Also, by keeping your content consistent both in regards to quality and time in terms of availability, you can create an incredibly positive feeling of anticipation among your viewers.

If you can come up with at minimum a month's worth of video content that you can upload two things. One, you can make the most of time. Remember the earlier chapter , I advised recording and editing multiple videos at once or edit to achieve more or use much less effort and time? There is no need to setup to shoot, pack, and set up for every video, as you can setup and shoot multiple videos and pack up to accomplish more in lesser time and effort.

Another benefit of having at minimum a month's worth videos on hand gives you a lot of flexibility. If you plan to upload videos, consider the next one, what you'll shoot next one, then shoot and upload on the following time, what happens if an emergency or urgent situation occurs? The scheduled shoot could need to be delayed, or even cancelled. In the end, you'll be not able to upload your content at the time people are looking forward to it. If this happens often you're likely to lose followers or at the very least, engaged ones. With one month's worth video content you'll have to spare yourself from the inevitable you encounter unexpected challenges and you'll still be posting quality content in a timely manner.

Communicate Your USP or Unique Selling Proposition

If people see you as identical to the others in your area, they'll not even bother to join your channel in the first place. You must give them an incentive to subscribe and, since you already have a reason having adhered to the guidelines in determining your segment, all you need to do is to communicate the reasons behind it - the channel's USP.

Be careful not to be explicit or obvious about it because the fact that you are explicit or overt about it will destroy the mystery or excitement over it. It is so "sales-y". The best method to do it is to do it in a subtle manner within your videos. This can be done by, for instance by mentioning, as an natural element in the dialogue in your videos, the purpose of your channel. This makes it appear authentic and isn't "sales-y" in the sense that you're aware of what I'm talking about.

Channel Persona

What I'm referring to is to give your YouTube channel a distinct or distinctive character. Although having a unique selling point is extremely helpful in building an army of engaged and loyal fans, having a distinctive and engaging can add character to your channel and videos can help build an even greater army!

It is possible to say that your channel is about personal finance. If not handled correctly, could be into boredom due to the mathematical and technical nature of the topic. One way to present an impressive image is to frame the subject in a fun and humorous way. You can as well compare financial concepts with commonplace - or even humorous - items. I think that's what most people mean by infotainment or information-entertainment. Information is easier to digest with a little element of entertainment. If your field of expertise allows it then do it. Sparky! Think about your most and least-favorite professors from the classroom and you'll understand the idea I'm trying to convey.

Annotate

Annotations refers to notes you could make on YouTube videos. These are extremely beneficial to increase your channel's following by following the steps:

"Spotlight": This kind of an annotation can be a clickable hyperlink that's embedded in your YouTube videos. It can be used to direct users to different YouTube video (yours or other) or to websites that enhance the information that you have posted on your video and offer your viewers an additional benefit for the time and effort spent watching your videos.

* Calls to Action: These are the statements that inform your viewers what you would like them to do following watching your videos. This could include, and not limited to, subscribing to your channel and viewing your videos, liking them, or your other channel's videos or sharing your content via social networks.

The great aspect of annotations is that you have an enormous amount of control over the way they appear. You can decide where on your video they'll be and the time they'll appear and when they'll disappear.

Feature Others' Channels

Another strategy to increase your YouTube advertising army is to scratching at other YouTube content creators on the back of their heads. By joining together with other content creators, you open your content to viewers of similar content creators. You can do this by incorporating special channels to your own.

By incorporating featured channels on your channel, you will be perceived by your viewers as someone who's confident in his or her own self-esteem enough to be able to promote other content of others and content. This confidence or feeling of security could be infectious and make your customers more confident and secure in your company, which can turn your viewers into loyal, devoted viewers.

How can I add channels that are featured? It's easy. Go through Modules, Other Channels, and then Save Changes that will allow Other Features on your channel. After that, you can add channels that you believe are similar to yours , and are beneficial to your audience. You can also save them. It's that simple!

Search Engine Optimization (SEO)

Another great method of increasing the number of viewers and, in turn engagement, in the process of gaining YouTube success is to use

SEO to create the descriptions of your videos and tags. SEO is an extensive subject to cover in this book, but simply stated SEO is the practice of using the appropriate keywords in the proper quantities in your online content (including the description and tags for YouTube videos) YouTube video) to help your content appear as prominent as it can on the result pages of the major search engines when you search for a certain keyword. The ultimate goal of SEO is having your content to be placed at high on the page of results for a specific keyword. The extent to which you can do SEO properly, you'll be able to ensure that those searching at your site's content or who are related to it, can be able to easily locate your videos.

Social Media Presence

If you are a fan of social media, and I'm guessing you are, then why not make use of your accounts to promote the YouTube channel you run and its videos? Although I wouldn't advise dispersing yourself too widely and jumping onto all social media platforms I would suggest picking one or two of those with the most members including Facebook, Twitter, and Instagram.

So , how do you optimize your social media platforms to increase traffic to the popularity of your YouTube channel? One way is to make sure you post content that isn't accessible on your channel, but closely related to the video or content. For instance, you can share behind-the-scenes videos as well as previews to the pages of your Facebook as well as Instagram accounts, and include the link to the video that you have on YouTube the source of these videos.

It is also possible to hold Facebook contests to help you promote your channel as well as your video content on YouTube. Contests are a great method to get people involved and the best part is that the fact that they're already engaged at time they visit your channel, meaning they're more likely of becoming extremely engaged subscribers. That's exactly the kind of subscribers you'll need for your channel.

Blogs

It could be difficult to grow the number of people who view your channel when your online presence is restricted to YouTube. There are millions of creators of video content on the market, as well as billions or more of videos that are competing for interest, you'll require every assistance you can get from other internet sources, such as blogs. Similar to your social media profiles making or using the already-existing blog of yours to advertise your YouTube channel is about posting posts and linking that assist in bringing users into the YouTube channel.

But why should you blog in the first place when you already have presence on social media? One reason is that blogs are more specific. Social media is about being social, and the content of which is generally more varied. Blogs allow you to concentrate on a specific subject or area that is ideal to attract loyal readers.

Another benefit blog sites have is you are able to publish more content, which is simpler to arrange. It's not easy to do the same thing on Facebook which is basically put according to chronological order. Blogs allow you to organize your content according to topics or sub-topics, or chronologically. The decision is yours.

Additionally, blogging is more effective for SEO when compared with social media. You can publish content that is can be more SEO-friendly on blogs than social media. As I said earlier, SEO is a great way to get more viewers who are interested in learning more about terms that are relevant to your video and channels.

If you believe that the blog you're writing on is highly-traffic one, one strategy you can increase visitors towards the YouTube channel and your YouTube videos is to use widgets. Here's how to do this:

To increase traffic to your blog and keep your visitors entertained while they are watching your YouTube videos, you can add your YouTube videos to your blog. This way, they are able to remain on your blog while they watch your videos. This decreases the chance of viewers being attracted by the other content on

YouTube when you direct viewers straight to the channel.

Install an YouTube subscriber widget to your website so that you are able to ask them to let them sign up to your YouTube channel without needing to go straight to your channel. This also helps the readers of your blog remain on your blog when they sign up to your channel. It also reduces the chance of them getting attracted by the other channels of YouTube.

...Then Monitor Your Channel's Performance

Most people don't plan at all but go gung ho. However, there are some who plan and follow through. But a small percentage are people who go that extra mile to be successful in keeping track of the progress. One way you can tell whether your strategies are effective and , if not, the reasons why is by keeping an eye on what's happening. There's a saying that if you do what you've always done, you'll always receive what you've always received. When you keep track of the performance of your YouTube channel, you can alter your approach to achieve different outcomes.

One crucial area that is a crucial part of the YouTube account that you'll have keep track of to determine whether you're doing a great job of reaching out to people who are interested in your content is your Audience Retention Report, which is accessible by clicking on the profile image in the upper right-hand corner of the homepage and then clicking on the box that says Creator Studio. It will take you to Your YouTube account's Dashboard that will show you, as well as other important statistics on your videos' analytics over the past 28 days. For a deeper review of the way your videos are performing by clicking the View All link at the bottom of the Analytics box that is on the left-hand side of your screen. Some of the most important information you will be able to access regarding your channel's capacity to attract and hold your viewers' the attention of viewers are total watch times as well as the average length of time viewers spend on your videos, as well as the how many views are viewed of your channel.

Particularly important in this case is the Average View Duration as it tells the viewer whether your viewers are increasingly interested in your content or whether they're getting bored. If the average time of viewing has increased, that simply indicates that your channel did better job maintaining the interest of viewers in comparison to the prior period. If it's been lower the likelihood is that it performed badly compared to the prior period.

In the section called Views In the Views section, you can view the number of people who watch the videos on your channel. It's an indication of how you've managed to market your content. It's all about reaching. If your total numbers of views for the month and your average duration were both lower in the month just ended this indicates that you've done an awful job running your YouTube channel during the period in question. A thorough strategy review should be considered if this is the situation.

Chapter 7: How Can Youtube Make You A Star?

The advent of social media as well as other types of social media has drastically changed the Internet in a similar way, almost in the same manner as the Internet has changed our lives.

Everyone can be the center of attention and present their views on life with an audience of all over the world due to YouTube as well as other platforms for social media. People now have accessibility, for the beginning, to huge audience previously restricted to the major TV networks and the well-off advertisers who favored these platforms. This does not mean that anyone is able to pick to the camera and achieve the fame and awe of an individual such as Walter Cronkite. On the contrary we all have the potential to use our own small area on YouTube to develop an audience and a following to share our unique view on life. It doesn't matter if make use of YouTube to share an opinion, promote our companies, or show our humor; the possibility of transforming our lives by sharing videos on demand is our hands and is completely within the medium.

1.1 A brief overview YouTube YouTube

It's not difficult to navigate or use YouTube because the folks who manage it have invested a lot of time to make it easy and easy to use. It shouldn't take much effort to find a video that is appealing to you on the home page of YouTube and is accessible via www.youtube.com.

First, you will see the videos in a row which are being watched by others. After that, you'll get a glimpse at the video that is being promoted, and then the videos that are featured will take up the largest portion of the page's first. You can click the links to view more featured Videos, the Most Viewed Videos as well as the most talked about videos and Top-Favorite Videos if there's nothing on the page that is interesting to you but we're confident that there's something that is sure to appeal to you. It may take a new user several times before they navigate past the homepage of the site.

You'll notice that there is a search bar that is empty. The box is inviting users to fill it in with your own interests to help you identify videos that are relevant to you. You can locate similar videos by searching every keyword(s) you could think of. You can decide if you'd like to look up channels or videos by using the pull-down function. The featured channels are similar with cable channel in that they focus on a particular subject and are limited in their scope of coverage.

When you search, you'll be able organize the results based on importance, relevance, date added as well as the number of times a video has been seen, and the grade that it was awarded from other YouTube users. If you've watched a video, finding other videos that are similar is easy. Videos that are similar to this one will be displayed on the right side and are accompanied by other videos that are similar to the source.

You can navigate to the channel, video and community areas of YouTube by clicking on the tabs at from the bottom of the page and which

YouTube calls"the watch" page. You can take a closer look at the details that are located under this tab. Community tab, in contrast towards tabs for Channel and Video. Video and Channel tabs, that both provide information.

There are a wide range of contests mostly run by businesses. Additionally, you'll find Groups which are groups in which people who share similar interests come together and share information. Finally, you've found The Community Help Forums.

1.2 A few words about YouTube the history of YouTube

YouTube, Web site for sharing videos. It was launched in February, 2005 by three people who previously worked for PayPal, the American online retailer PayPal. The names of the three were Steve Chen, Chad Hurley as well as Jawed Karim. The company's headquarters are within San Bruno, California, and was established with the idea that normal people would enjoy the distribution of videos of their "home footage."

The site was launched during May of 2005 and was initially accessible on a limited basis, referred to by the name of "beta," and by June of the same year it was receiving around 30000 visitors every day. At the time YouTube was officially launched to the general public on December 15th in 2005, the site had already been in the process of generating more than 2 million video views per day. This had risen to over 25 million viewers by the time January 2006 arrived. As of the month March, 2006 the number of movies that could be watched on the site grew to nearly 25 million plus more than 20,000 brand new movies were posted each day. At the time of the end of the year, YouTube was already providing more than 100 million video clips per every day. The pace of new movies uploaded to the site did not show any sign of slowing down.

1.3 What can YouTube make you a celebrity?

Every day, a brand new YouTube phenomenon is born. Being a YouTube star as fast as you can is creating a video seen by millions of viewers around the globe. The definition of a viral video however it's not a standard-fits-all project. The most well-known videos on YouTube tend to be just an unplanned action of imagination by the creator. This is a possibility, however it can be challenging. Fans and friends of your channel on YouTube are most likely to watch your videos. Therefore, you are more likely to become a YouTube celebrity if you've got an impressive following.

Contact other YouTubers who create and share videos with the same topics like yours to increase your reach. People are more likely to reciprocate and check out your video if they make the effort to like and leave comments on their videos.

A YouTube channel that is official serves as a platform to establish yourself as an emerging star in the field of video on the internet. The content on your YouTube channel should be designed in a way that it is quickly crawled in search engines.

When you regularly add new videos or different content onto your YouTube channel by providing your viewers with the incentive to visit your channel regularly. If you're an YouTube celebrity it is possible to increase your reach. Your videos need to be seen to become an YouTube famous. In order for your videos to be watched in the first place, they have to be found. If you're hoping to be a YouTube celebrity you can benefit from the advice of others who are YouTube celebrities. Create a list of YouTubers that you love their videos and are well-known. Follow them by making comments on the videos of these YouTubers, as well as becoming friends with them.

You'll meet with people from the entertainment industry who will help you build your own superstar status by offering tips and connections the networks they have.

In order to help you become to become a YouTube celebrity, ensure that your videos are tagged with relevant keywords and descriptions.

The guidelines for YouTube are strictly followed by the celebrities who use the platform. Infractions could lead to them being removed from the site.

The most important rule is to not violate copyright laws on the videos you upload and also to have a good relationship with your fellow YouTubers.

Chapter 8: What Is The Best Way To Market Yourself From Youtube?

We've heard from lots of people who've had success with YouTube due to their search ways to develop a passion or start a small business or to create an audience which could lead to employment or other opportunities within the world of work. Professionals who encourage those seeking jobs to utilize YouTube to advertise their resumes and also students in high school who credit their YouTube videos for aiding them in climbing the ranks of applicants to college who were initially turned down. YouTube is not just a platform where you can enjoy yourself It's an extremely effective instrument that can be used by anyone who wishes to understand how to use it. To be acquainted with these pioneers, first we must know the people they represent.

Writers, performers, artists business people, and even people who aren't celebrities are all within this category. Even if some individuals in this group were simply out to party but now have corporate managers and advertising agencies that are looking to protect their interests.

2.1 Performing

The majority of the time was filled with performers who were aspiring, however, very few were able to make it to the highest levels.

There were a small individuals successful in achieving their dream who could make the jackpot and make a decent living from it. This is because it's accurate comedy stand-up in the evening, a taxi driver in the daytime. All that has changed since the invention of YouTube. There are many comedians that have, despite not being nominated for a spot at the Hollywood Walk of Fame, have been able to provide for their families and friends with the popularity they've earned through YouTube. A lot of these comedians take on auditions or job prospects with evidence of their popularity to the public and also achieving their financial goals via placements in products and YouTube collaborations.

The most important thing to do is to choose your career in a field you love. Performers on YouTube can reach an almost unlimited audience, and it's possible to create a area of interest and also attract others who are interested in the same things. It is essential to prove that your content is an audience that is large enough to persuade the decision makers who will sign the checks are issued, regardless of regardless of whether you're dealing with traditional media such as books or broadcasting on television. Making it into the field takes a lot of time. But, the cost of creating uploading, distributing, and sharing personal content to YouTube is low enough that you are able to play around and discover the best solution for your needs.

Tips for becoming a top YouTuber YouTube

* Determine your strengths

* Post videos continuously

Be sure to monitor your audience's behavior and identify common questions you are able to answer on your videos.

* Create a unique production style

* Make a clear call to share your cards and screens at the end

Make use of an artist studio to boost visibility of videos

* Promote your channel and your content through other social platforms

2.2 YouTube teachers

YouTube videos that teach YouTube that teach users how to complete something are usually one of the top seen content. No matter if you're seeking to learn to play guitar, improve your mileage on gas or even how to get an excellent haircut, YouTube is certain to provide what you're looking for.

Learn your target audience. Who are you hope to persuade?

Analyzing the videos with the most views or that are ones that are most popular on the site on which you're publishing content is the best way to find out this information. This will give you an accurate idea of who your target audience are as well as what kind of content they like to consume. There's a wide range of choices available and you could be amazed by the number of music subgenres with a large audience. There's a wide variety in music people love listening to.

Create a captivating video.

This requires an engaging narrative with music, lighting and editing options. On the Internet it's true that the less you have, the better. you have only just a few seconds to capture an attention from your viewers and you must draw them in right away and get on the right track as fast as you can. The quality of your production is equally important. Of of course, not all people have the necessary skills to be a professional videographer, however you must do your best. Research diverse video approaches. It is your objective to know as much as you can about the process of creating videos. It's always beneficial to look at your work by the eyes of a novice viewer (especially in the case of being engrossed in your project for a long duration) Don't be unwilling to ask family members and friends to share their thoughts. If you make the effort to make improvements, you'll see a huge change in a very small amount of time.

Be sure to give an excellent first impression.

If users visit sites for videos they choose what video to watch according to its description and the thumbnail picture.

Both of these could be significant in the extent to which your video will be. To get people to view the link, there must be something that catches their attention. You'll only succeed if your first impression gives a clear impression of what they're likely to experience once they begin to watch. A good description should be one that sums up the event in a few paragraphs, and using as few words as is possible.

Imagine this as the title of your video. If you're given the choice of selecting a thumbnail image for your video, choose one that provides the most accurate image of the video and will entice viewers to view it. Keep communication open and be easily accessible. Include the URL of your personal site either on the video or the descriptions they accompany when you have one. There are many video sites which offer players that can be integrated on other websites which allows you to draw users from your website to theirs, and reverse the process.

Profit from this chance.

Also, you should include your contact number on the site or on your videos. It will be easier for those who appreciate your work to communicate with you. This can give your video an intimate appearance. As a result, viewers can feel closer to your video's creator, which could help in promoting spread of the video. When you establish acquaintances with people from different backgrounds You should start putting together an email list with individuals whom you are able to contact when you've got new content to present to them.

2.3 Video Resumes

You're probably aware that we share a deep love for video content in general, and YouTube specifically. It was natural that initially it seemed to us as if it would be an excellent idea to promote oneself in the course of your next job search through YouTube. It is possible to wear your best attire and work on your presentation skills and let potential employers see you in action in order to see firsthand how you present. It wasn't until we spoke to professionals working in human resources (HR) and recruitment managers that we discovered that it's not as simple as it appeared at first. We've come to the awareness that video resumes could be difficult to navigate and can even hinder the efforts of a person to find work. Many HR professionals dislike them.

Potential Legal Troubles

There is a possibility of being considered discriminatory in the event that one evaluates prospective employees on the basis of their appearance. Video footage gives an opportunity to get distracted by insignificant information, like hairstyles or clothes fashion, even though your goal isn't to disqualify the person.

The Incorrect First Impression

It's difficult to look natural and give the impression you're looking for, especially if you've no prior experience in front of cameras and aren't at ease doing it. If you're creating videos for YouTube there will be an area you'd like to focus your attention around and will be occupied with delivering your message to your viewers. Selling yourself is a totally different undertaking. If you make a bad performance on video , and it's shared on the Internet and it is shared widely, it won't be able to help your chances of landing the job you're looking for right now, but it could continue to follow you around for quite a while after it.

Time Restriction

Many employers claim that they only have around 10 seconds to read an applicant's resume is really embarrassing to consider when considering the amount of time needed to create a resume. So, they don't have the possibility of viewing the contents of a video. Additionally the search for keywords cannot be conducted on video as is the method used by the majority of companies utilize to find potential candidates. If your data isn't put into databases and searched with keywords, there's an excellent possibility that it won't be considered by the company who is hiring.

Chapter 9: Marketing Your Company On Youtube

Your life is able to be transformed by YouTube. However it is more likely that you'll choose to use YouTube to further the goals of a company that is already established instead of pursuing an employment as the video producer. That's great and we're able to assist you in this regard. Businesses of all sizes selling anything from soaps to software have been successfully using the video hosting website YouTube to market their services, increase brand and product awareness, and create new revenue. This should not come as a surprise considering the rapid growth YouTube has seen around the globe in recent years.

We'll turn our attention to companies and organizations who are actively exploring the possibilities that are offered by YouTube. There are many examples of businesses that have been successful on YouTube for nearly every kind of industry you can imagine. But, to be successful on YouTube requires a blend of science and art with equal amounts.

3.1 Videos that are most effective

"Video in demand" refers to the actions that users of YouTube are doing when they watch videos on the site. They don't want to be a victim of clicking at an advertisement regardless of whether they do not like the advertisements which accompany certain videos since they know that ads are necessary to ensure that the site remains free. But, they might be okay with ads that are accompanied by other films. If this is the situation the viewers will continue to click as fast as their fingers permit them. If you're considering making video content for your business be aware that it's advantageous if the video is designed to entertain first and then marketing later.

It is possible to believe that the most effective way to know the best way to join YouTube is to spend endless hours browsing the site to find out what other companies are doing. But this isn't the scenario. Although it's a good practice to be aware of the competition on a constant basis You may find that your time should be to think about your own company its products and services, the types of products it offers, the kinds of clients it serves and the goals that you set for reaching these customers via the videos they create.

You're in the best position to understand the character of your client base and consequently the type of strategy that appeals to them the most all is the kind of approach you adopt.

The following list is intended to provide an understanding of the kind of video content the most well-liked on YouTube so that you can place your videos within these categories. If you'd like your video to succeed it is best to make content that falls within one of these categories.

Videos of Products Being Reviewed

Reviews that you can rely on are more essential than ever prior to making purchases. The majority of customers aren't likely to make purchases without checking reviews on various sites first. Review of products goes further than online reviews by providing viewers with the chance to see how the product works and also get commentary on the product from the individual who designed it. It's no as a surprise to find that among the viewed type of video on YouTube is in this type of format.

Tutorial Video Clips

The majority of beauty influencers' content is comprised of instructional videos. This format is discussed in depth by a large variety of channels with millions of subscribers. Videos that show viewers how to accomplish something are very popular since they provide the perfect combination of knowledge and practical use.

Vlogs

Because of the people's aversion to the authentic video format Vlog channels are regularly receiving many millions of people watching. A lot of beauty influencers are vlogging on the channels they run (some may even own a separate channel for vlogging) and say they have had a lot of success with the content they share on their videos.

Gaming Videos

Gaming videos are among the most watched videos on YouTube, even though beauty industry isn't the intended users for this particular subgenre. If you're one who loves playing games on video, then launching an online gaming channel is an awesome idea.

Videos of Comedy Sketches

People love to laugh a lot. Research suggests that comedy videos may be the highest likely kind of video content that will be deemed "viral." Many beauty experts have integrated the skit formula in their videos as engaging introductions that were precisely designed.

Haul Videos

The beauty-focused producers on YouTube are the main reason behind the rise of this format and is still among the top-rated videos on the market currently. Additionally, the haul videos are extremely popular with companies that rely on them as a simple method to showcase their latest products to customers.

Favorites/Best Of Videos

Another form of video that is extremely popular with people who make content that is related to style and fashion is the Vlog. The videos that are most liked by viewers offer an intimate view of the things the YouTuber really likes and currently using. This is an important element that can influence the purchase choice made by customers.

Educational Videos

The viewers who watch YouTube videos YouTube are searching for something that is valuable, therefore it should not come as a shock that instructional videos have become among of the most watched video formats. You can easily add instructional films to your repertoire if you have an online fashion or beauty channel that is on YouTube. Videos that cover issues like cosmetic ingredients as well as ethical fashion labels as well as the history behind certain trends or styles as well as a range of other subjects are extremely popular with viewers.

3.2 Making money through YouTube

It's possible that earning money from YouTube isn't the primary reason to start a channel, however, being amazed by the variety of ways to earn money is a pleasant experience. It's good to know that making money from YouTube can be accomplished in many different creative ways.

Your followers could be your crucial factor to unlocking the revenue opportunities for the YouTube channel, which is the norm for Instagram influencers and bloggers. But the creation of a variety of revenue streams either through business ventures or side hustles is the way you earn money.

Join YouTube Partner Program by signing up. YouTube Partner Program by signing up.

Advertising is probably going be the initial source of income you look into. Signing up to YouTube's YouTube Partner Program and establishing the possibility of monetizing your channel is a vital action to consider in order to earn money through YouTube whether as a content creator or someone who does not upload content.

You'll need to prove that you are in compliance with all YouTube's regulations regarding monetization and that you are residing in a region or country which has accessibility to YouTube Partner Program. Once you have reached the threshold of 1,000 subscriber and 4000 watching hours during the year prior you'll be able to apply to monetize your account.

Promote the sales of items or products.

You can access many different items which can be offered for sale through your YouTube channel to earn money for you. Selling merchandize items such as t-shirts coffee mugs, bags for totes snapbacks, etc. on, can be beneficial as well as financial benefits.

Your online profile and brand are now visible in the real world due to merchandise. This will not only increase the reach of your followers but also enhances the bond that you have with your fans since they can "invest" in the work you're doing by buying your products.

It's much easier to market branded products than what it might appear to be initially. With freelancing marketplaces such as Fiverr You can make orders for affordable designs that can be customized to specific products, like T-shirts.

In terms of managing orders, you could integrate your shop with services like DSers or any of the other print-on-demand companies that manage delivery, fulfillment as well as customer service. This allows you to benefit from all the advantages of a print-on demand business, and put in considerably less effort for yourself. The DSers service is an instance of a service that falls into this category.

Fund your next creative endeavor using crowdsourcing.

Crowdfunding is an excellent option to look into in situations where the sole obstacle to the idea from going into practice is the lack of funds.

If you need assistance to purchase more equipment, hiring actors, or reimbursing other costs of production, you can seek contributions from both your audience as well as the community of people connected to crowdfunding, provided that your campaign is appealing enough.

You might consider making a video that outlines your idea or giving an idea of what the project could be like, because the majority of successful crowdfunded creative projects typically offer an initial glimpse or "trailer" which gets people interested. It is something to be thinking about doing when your project is set to be a crowdfunded project.

Your audience should be given the opportunity to support you financially with "fan finance."

It is also possible to create "fan raising" streams that allow you to get financial donations from your fans in a manner similar to crowdfunding.

As an artist, you are making your voice heard online without having your viewers to pay for a subscription to hear or view the content you create. So, if you're giving your viewers top-quality content, they might find it appealing to them to follow your work on a regular basis.

Offer to license your content to different media outlets.

You might be able to licence your content to others in exchange of financial rewards if you are able to make an online video that goes popular and has appeal to the masses for example, like an entertaining video of your dog.

If your videos get popular enough to be considered viral, numerous media outlets such as morning shows, internet news websites, as well as other producers of content may reach them to discuss rights to utilize them.

Furthermore, you also can also list your videos on markets, like Trusted Media Brands, where it is easier for those with the proper credentials to find and purchase your content.

Many platforms that allow crowd funding for content producers provide them with an additional platform on which their work and also a means to engage their most loyal fans and express their gratitude to them for their loyalty.

Work with various businesses to be an influencer.

Advertising costs that are typically large on influential personalities who have already earned the respect of their followers is becoming a more well-known trend for companies. This trend can be observed in the growth of influencer sponsorships and marketing.

If you're an artist and are capable of negotiating the right terms, you stand with a huge chance.

Join an affiliate marketing business.

The possibility of earning a commission from the marketing of a product or service offered by a different firm could be an instance of affiliate-marketing. You can be an affiliate marketer for various companies and include endorsements, product placements or other types of media into your marketing plan. However, you must to inform the viewers of your content aware of these collaborations.

This approach can be particularly successful when you make use of the power of your YouTube channel to post reviews of products. It's usually not hard to start since the risk isn't from the company (they only pay when they sell) So the hurdle to entry is very low.

Chapter 10: Making Youtube Videos

This is the final chapter has been in the making throughout the years. Now it's a given that you're eager to get out your video camera and begin recording footage, aren't you? All you've learned up to now should be flowing through your mind like water. Thus, you should be prepared to receive the final instructions that you will need before you begin to stake your claim on the world of YouTube. You'll get many helpful ideas knowledge, facts, and tips on the process of creating your own videos that are successful for YouTube. Instead, we'll give you the wisdom of some of the most successful video makers. These are two essential aspects you have to be aware of.

Preplanning.

It's moment to put on your thinking cap and allow your imagination run free. How do you imagine the final video? What do you envision it to appear like? Once you've got your concept in your mind it is important to break the project down into steps that can be managed. This is not only to be able to be aware of what you must do following, but also to ensure you can collect all the equipment, set-ups, people and props prior to when you begin to work to complete the task.

The video is being put together.

Now, you will be able to start recording and learn in a the hands-on way how to present your personal story via video. Before you move on to the next step it is essential to ensure that step one is completed in full. Even after a few attempts at creating a video you'll see the difference that careful preplanning can bring about. You'd like to feel that you're gaining valuable information with every video you create although it's likely that your first attempts won't be huge success. The more you plan ahead, the greater chance that this is the situation. Be aware that careful editing is necessary during this phase of the process. Editing is the process that converts the raw video footage narrative.

4.1 Things you're facing

Alongside the usual "noise" which is the norm for living in the twenty-first century, you'll also need to compete with other creators of videos on YouTube to attract the attention of people who view your videos. Residents of New York Metropolis do not need to deal with the constant background noise which is an integral element of living in the city. And we're not talking about the annoying neighbor who keeps awakes the entire neighborhood by launching his leaf blower at 7:15 on the morning of a Saturday. We believe that regardless of where you live we are constantly exposed to a plethora of messages and information that are all competing to grab our attention. This is the case regardless of the media through which the message or information is communicated. Since we're constantly bombarded with a variety of thoughts going through our heads simultaneously it's difficult to keep track of everything happening around us.

They are all competing with you, and we're not even including your spouse, wife or partner, children, pets, work and civic associations or household responsibilities! Now you should have an understanding of there are a myriad of compelling reasons to ensure that your videos are viewed by the right people. It's not the blame of the majority people who have attention spans similar to those of fly's. It's just the way things have changed due to people getting used to the constant flow of information. The problem of having a limited attention span is particularly prevalent in younger generations who spend their whole life surfing the Internet and are affluent in huge amounts on YouTube. Remember that even after you have found your content on YouTube and is watching it the millions of other videos one click away to view.

4.2 Research and objectives

Most users make money out their YouTube content by receiving a large amount of attention, also referred to as a large number of views. If you've got a huge variety of opinions, a range of outcomes can be expected. The partnership with YouTube is just one of the possibilities. As you've probably guessed, YouTube partners can generate income from advertisements displayed on the webpage that YouTube utilizes to show its videos. You could also create an online site or microsite that your customers can go to in order to take the desired task for example, buying your products. This type of site is called"landing spot" or a "landing place." When you begin to prepare the video, the first question you need to consider is "What do I would like the viewers of my video to experience after they're done the video?" This is the initial stage in the process of planning. The answer to this question differs based on the goals of the creator. With an understanding of the steps to build an effective YouTube channel we can take a look at some specific examples of success to find out what the ultimate objectives were.

So, there's many reasons to use YouTube as a platform, and it's quite possible that your motive isn't included in this list. But before you begin making your videos you must know what you're trying to achieve by the videos. At a minimum you need to determine the purpose behind your first video prior to creating them.

This is valid even if the goal changes as you upload more video and gain knowledge.

To date the most debate has been centered around the nature of YouTube and the kind of content that seems to be well-liked on the platform. What does this issue connect to what you believe is right for you and the type of videos you'd like to upload to YouTube that are your own? You may also look for channels that might be relevant to you, and you've already begun integrating yourself with YouTube. YouTube community. It is likely that you have seen a lot of video content in your education. You've got enough experience to be able to grasp a good understanding of the functions on the website and you should be at this moment. However, since we're trying to push ourselves so let's be even more specific on what we're talking about. Below are some tactics that have proved to be successful on YouTube.

4.3 Storyboards

You've gathered you team (or at the very least, you've) You are ready to put on your hoodie and start working. What should we do now? A storyboard is a good place to begin in narrating what you intend to be the "narrative" in your movie. At this point, when you actually plan an elongated board that is that resembles comic books to display each scene you're planning to shoot when you tell your story.

How will you inform the reader about the setting of your story? Which is your minimum amount of characters required to accomplish this? What extent will your characters require costumes and props? When you start constructing your plot , one section at each time, these details become clearer and distinct.

If you don't own it, all the basic equipment and tools will be required for your initial projects are usually within reach. It is also necessary to have some sort editing software in addition to a video camera or camera. There may be additional lighting, based on the lighting setting you select for the initial video you record. It will require the laptop or computer that you've been working with during the entire process to navigate YouTube. The need that people have for digital video to be recorded in a convenient and easy way has definitely been recognized by the makers of video cameras. There is a good chance that your phone comes with this feature. Most of the time an inexpensive digital camera or camcorder is needed to begin however there are a few instances where this is not the case. As your proficiency grows and you begin working on productions that are becoming more difficult, you'll have the option of buying additional equipment.

4.4 Filming your videos

While it can seem to give off a sense of seriousness A script can actually be an extremely useful instrument that can aid you to maintain your focus. You must ensure that you have all of the visuals (shots and angles, graphics and so on.) prepared prior to recording the dialog. When you have already written a blog article on something, you might want to think about making a script inspired by the blog post rather than creating a new script. It's not necessary to be complex. If you think it's too much effort to be a necessity an outline of the basics can aid you in understanding your points

, and is superior to beginning the recording process without having a plan.

If you are recording yourself among essential things you need to avoid is having a lot of clutter in and out of the camera. If you're filming at work or in your workplace or at your home, you'll want the environment to be clean and tidy.

Then, you'll have to alter the video's illumination and your webcam or camera (if you own these). For video with higher quality, you can either utilize an external webcam which is connected to your laptop more importantly transform a single lens digital reflex camera to webcam.

If you are taking photos of yourself, ensure that everything you see on your screen is clean and free of distracting elements. If you're not able to access an entire wall in one color that is uncluttered which creates a stunning backdrop. But should that not be an alternative, just make sure your surroundings is as clear as it is.

You wish for the attention of your visitors to be directed towards your work, not towards the piece which is on your wall.

If your video contains a screen record or screen capture, then the mess on your computer's screen can be as distracting on the camera's screen. Nothing is more irritating than having to search through useless programs and apps to locate the material you would like to include in your film.

If you're recording in front of windows, make sure you aren't recording on the other side of the window. Set yourself in a spot in which you are able to see through the window or close to it. It's not like you appear drained or look like a silhouette if you approach it this way. One word of caution: this is an excellent way to enhance the light in your space but you must be extremely cautious as it isn't easy to control the quantity of light.

Make adjustments to the tilt of the webcam to ensure that it is close to the eye of your audience. This will keep your audience from having to stare at you. Use the guidelines by the

Rule of Thirds, or place yourself in the middle of the image.

Chapter 11: Youtube Revenue System

YouTube isn't only a great source of entertainment but it's also a huge phenomenon in the world of culture. It's something millions of people are exposed to regularly. The remaining question is: can you earn money from YouTube? The biggest challenge is achieving financial success. There are a variety of ways to earn money through YouTube videos that have proven to work.

First and foremost is what is it that means"to "make profits"? YouTube videos can certainly help in the sale of products as well as services. It is just one of the ways companies can earn money. However, there's also a benefit of having your name dragged into the eyes to thousands of people positively. This contributes to the effectiveness of your marketing efforts that should also be taken into consideration as "earning cash." So too should the cash you will save on customer support or recruitment, as well as other forms of marketing because from your successful use of video on the internet.

The Internet has witnessed a dramatic change within a relatively short period of time. Although the amount that can be earned from video on the internet may not be significant in the present however, who is willing to argue that the number of people who watch it will grow by an exponential rate? Our society is completely obsessed with video. Additionally, we enjoy an increased degree of control and an array of choices in our preferred means of entertainment due to the Internet.

5.1 YouTube Partner Program

Creators who are on YouTube are now able to access enhanced tools, opportunities, and additional features as a result through this YouTube partnership program. All you need is a channel, a few videos to be broadcast and the correct target audience.

This feature is great for YouTube creators who wish to make money from YouTube channels. YouTube channels with minimal of effort, thanks to the launch the feature.

It is free of cost, and participation is entirely voluntary for the creators who are on the platform.

There are numerous benefits to joining the YouTube partner program, however the aspect that Google handles all the management on your behalf is perhaps the most important. It could be the placing of advertisements or the collection of payments and revenues. Google manages everything. This is why it offers a safe and secure method of monetization through YouTube.

It is possible that the channel will encounter the following three important events when it has been accepted into YouTube's YouTube partnership program

A banner display advertisement of which it is usually described as an "overlay in-video ad" may be placed inside the window.

Before the beginning of the original video it is possible that a small commercial similar to TV commercials could be broadcast.

The banner ads automatically begin playing when you visit a channel's homepage on YouTube.

If someone views, clicks on, or watches the video ad playing on the channel's website the business begins receiving income for the event.

The amount of money earned by a channel varies from one channel, and is affected by several variables, including the type of advertisement viewers engaged with and the length of time they watched it.

Channels are able to boost their revenue by increasing the quantity of relevant content they have on their website and having the content published.

The idea of cooperation between channel administrators in YouTube and Google is a key element to Google's general strategy.

5.2 Selling via landing pages

WordPress is a system for managing content that lets users create more than only websites. It is possible to start providing the possibility of landing pages to your clients and this is something you can start before you create an online solution or even make it an option for certain types of campaigns. In any situation, landing pages possess the potential to create an impact on the performance of a business. It is vital to be familiar with the method of selling this product.

Imagine someone is watching your video uploaded to YouTube at the moment. In essence, they've entered your store via the front door. For the moment you have full control over the process. Your goal is to make sure your video is engaging or entertaining enough that viewers will enjoy the whole thing and will be intrigued to know more about you and your company. How can you convert that potential customer into an income source for your business? In a different way ask yourself, what exactly is it that you want them to do following watching the video? The idea of directing visitors to an online landing page, or microsite is among the most commonly used methods for turning viewers into customers (discussed in a moment). We have briefly discussed landing pages before however now we'll look at the concept in greater detail.

Microsites are an alternative to a landing pages that has gained popularity with those who make videos online. It's a website that is specifically designed which was designed to help support an online video marketing campaign.

5.3 Video Advertising

The video you upload can also earn advertising revenues. The popularity of online video advertising has grown and has become more complicated. It's not just about web ads. Ad fatigue in the pre-roll is a concern. Advertisers may run these ads on your site with convincing arguments.

Google AdWords generates most of Google's revenues. Google's algorithm produces search results that range from weather to finance. In addition to the search results the AdWords marketer can also suggest related websites. AdWords advertisements are found on almost every Google websites. AdWords provides suggestions on Gmail, YouTube, Google Maps and many other Google websites. Advertisers have to bid higher than one another for the most prominent Google spots. The higher the bid, the more expensive it is. bids that are low may not be displayed.

Advertising companies pay Google for each click. Search terms that are extremely competitive like insurance, loans and others financial offerings, may earn a few cents up to $50 or more per click.

When Google purchased YouTube it was expected that problems with copyrights to be addressed and that advertising would be added. YouTube copyright issues concern how the service can protect the creators' exclusive rights in reproduction and rights. YouTube has been the subject of numerous copyright cases over the years, however advertisers initially were strong.

As the stream of user-generated content increased in every day, advertisers were exposed to an excessive amount of inappropriate content. Advertising rates dropped as advertisers reverted to search ads which were viewed by consumers as they were researching the possibility of making a purchase.

Google has a range of YouTube options for expanding the YouTube channel. One option is a monthly subscription to an advertisement-free YouTube with original videos. In the autumn of 2015. YouTube began offering YouTube Red the $9.99-a-month subscription that provides ads-free music and videos without interruptions.

YouTube Premium and YouTube Music were changed on May 17, 2018. YouTube Music is free with commercials, however a subscription level allows for ad-free playback, audio-only background playback, as well as offline downloads.

YouTube Premium along with YouTube Music Premium give users the option of a trial period for one month at $11.99 per month until 2021.

YouTube plans to stop ads in video, which earn no revenue. The website wants to push companies to join existing ad networks instead of having YouTube stars make deals with outside parties. This dangerous move may force creators of content to other platforms, while also closing the YouTube advertisement loophole.

The biggest issue with YouTube appears to be the fact that it is attracting the most direct viewers. A lot of users are just browsing through embeds or just popping into YouTube for a few videos without doing any clicks. YouTube hopes to become an alternative destination site to combat this by giving Google the opportunity to earn money from videos.

5.4 Leveraging your videos

Once you've made a name for yourself on YouTube and uploaded your videos, the content you upload on YouTube could generate other income streams. You may not make a decision to sell anything related to your videos However, there are alternative alternatives, which are less obvious, to earn money from the content you create. Once you've reached the point of being successful, you will be able to earn money.

There are plenty of financially successful YouTube businesses that are raking in steady incomes through the platform. Much less effort was devoted in the marketing of its products and services by entrepreneurs who were the pioneers of the first generation.

The number of firms offering consulting services is likely to increase dramatically as a consequence of the growing amount of competition in this industry. In this case, then you have to be more assertive in your marketing your business. Make sure to include the link to your Channel page that directs users to your website or microsite. There, you can provide additional information about the ways you can aid your viewers.

5.5 Sponsorships for promotions

The most important weapon that marketing has in its arsenal is influencers and content creators.

It is evident the fact that YouTube is the largest social network for making purchases on the internet! Advertising on YouTube are becoming more popular for companies as a means to advertise their goods.

Sponsorship deals are the most effective method of revenue generation in the case of YouTube content providers operating smaller channels.

Instead of investing in traditional advertising, companies are putting more than ever in partnerships paid for.

They'll receive the highest-quality attention in the event that they appear to your page. Actually an analysis conducted by Google found it was found that YouTube productions were four times more efficient than celebrities in establishing recognition for a brand.

It's time to begin making money from the value of your YouTube channel if an artist or content creator with an following through the channel. To begin all you need is a strong brand offering and obtaining one is far easier than you imagine it to be.

Businesses can enhance their business practices by creating partnerships with strategic content suppliers. They can draw in an increased number of consumers and build trust in their products as a result of this. If you've spent time and energy the growth of your following on YouTube and you're in a great place to start developing an additional source of income.

Payment-based sponsorships are not just more sustainable but also place you in the control of your own revenues.

5.6 YouTube screen room

Independent filmmakers and distributors have the opportunity to generate cash through the use of YouTube's Screening Room, which may be found at www.youtube.com/ytscreeningroom. Every Friday, YouTube plays four films for viewers to take a look at. Most of the movies displayed within the Screening Room have already been shown at film festivals taking place globally.

Furthermore, there's the latest information available and that is where the possibility of earning money is a factor with respect to this scenario (so to say). It is widely believed it is YouTube is the sole entity that pays the cost of the original materials. (Since the advertisements cost a lot of money are shown on that site and are displayed on the page, it is probable that it is true. Exposure alone will not be enough to satisfy many of the filmmakers, the majority of them have probably already enjoyed some kind of success. As we went into the Screening Room, one of the films playing was Ascension The film that received the award for the Best Film in the Science Fiction and Fantasy Film Festival in 2008.

You must watch videos in the Screening Room using the specialized video player available at the location that will give you the most optimal viewing experience. If your company is an independently owned producer and/or distributor, it's suggested to reach out to YouTube for more details. YouTube Screening Room can be reached by e-mail at ytscreeningroom@youtube.com.

5.7 YouTube's competitors

A number of video-sharing sites, such as Revver, Metacafe, and Flixya are emerging as alternative in the wake of YouTube in recent times. They've searched YouTube to determine who is most popular, and then sought out some of the most popular YouTube stars with the hope of forming lucrative revenue-sharing agreements with these sites. This approach was particularly successful during the times when YouTube was not yet able to implement its own similar program in place. Revver is especially generous, at the moment of this writing giving contributors a portion of 50 percent of any advertising revenues earned by their films. It's no shock to learn that YouTube has lost major users to other platforms. This includes comedians who go under the name Smosh and LonelyGirl15.

5.8 Effectivity of your videos

Being able to measure the effectiveness of an advertising campaign is among the most essential elements of any marketing plan which is why online-based video shouldn't be a exception to this standard. YouTube along with Google Analytics are two platforms that can assist with this. The reason for this is simple: if you are aware of areas that you are struggling in, you'll be able improve not only the quality of your content, but also the manner in which that it's distributed. If you are aware of areas where you are doing well in the YouTube ranking, you will also know the areas where you have to focus your efforts.

Demographics

This section will provide you details on the gender, age and the locations that your audience members are. Why is it important to consider this? The first step is to do an analysis to determine if you're reaching your target customers. If most of your viewers are under 40, even though most of your customers could be middle-aged women who are in their forties it is possible that your strategy for content needs some rethinking. You should however, consider the factors that led to the video's popularity with younger generations. It is possible that there is an opportunity that you've not thought about using.

Playback position

This report will let you know which of your films are watched online, whether they're being watched directly through YouTube or as embedding on different sites. On YouTube it is possible to find out if your videos have seen on either the view page (the actual URL on which the video was uploaded) or the channel's page. It is also possible to determine when you've started an Google advertisement campaign or YouTube advertisement and if viewers are viewing your video via it.

The amount of time spent watching and the percentage of viewers that are on average

Additionally additional tab, the one on right will show the proportion of the footage that is observed while it is being replayed. The average view time gives details about the length of time a video has been played on an average, in seconds. Keep a close eye on these important parameters. While there are plenty of people who are just focused on the number of views and views, these are the factors and several others which help your video get more highly on YouTube. If they're significantly less than you expected and you are not sure, pay close at the analysis below.

Audience retention

You are able to collect information about a particular video at a variety of times. You can also track when your viewers quit your videos. It's possible they've not realized the information they were seeking and that's why they left quickly in the event that they had. If that's the case the title of your movie or the thumbnail may be unclear for viewers. Consider this If they stopped watching afterward: Did they lost interest? Did you find that specific part difficult to understand? It's also possible to simply created the content on a YouTube card on your site that connects to your site and directs visitors to the site. If you observe specific spikes in the chart, this means that viewers have viewed that particular portion of content several times. A drop in viewers could mean that people skim over certain parts.

The tab that is the absolute audience retention is where you'll get all this data but the relative audience retention is an fascinating statistic you can utilize to assess the level of engagement your video has. If you compare it to similar videos posted on YouTube with similar length the ability of a video to keep viewers entertained is assessed in terms of the "relative viewer retention." This graphic is simple and makes easy to determine if your results differ from the normal.

The reasons for traffic

This report gives a detailed breakdown of the various ways how your viewers could have accessed your video through YouTube. This includes YouTube search and suggest YouTube videos, Explore features playlists YouTube channels and YouTube advertising, as well as other options.

Devices The section on devices will inform you the number of people who watched your video via a mobile phone tablet, desktop computer. You'll be able to offer a more enjoyable experience for users when you consider the video's format, aspect ratio, as well as the surroundings in which they're viewing your video.

Engagement reports

You will find them within the part of the document called "Overview." Clicking on each name, you'll get access to additional options and data that are more extensive about these metrics.

- Views

It is a crucial measure of the quality of your videos , considering the total amount of times that a video has been watched.

- Likes and Dislikes

It's also an important indicator that will provide you with data about the level of engagement of your target audience. It's normal to get some minor dislikes, however, if you observe that the number of negative reviews are increasing, it is time to consider reevaluating your content and determine if you're reaching your intended people using the metrics listed in the previous paragraph.

- Shares

This information reveals the amount of times your video was shared by YouTube users through the "Share" button and also the sites that users use to post your video (e.g. Facebook, Tumblr, and Blogger). Additionally, you can gain access to data that is specific to specific websites.

Comments are not only an excellent gauge of audience engagement They also offer an avenue by where you can seek feedback from the audience. Keep in mind that some kinds of videos usually draw more comments than other categories do. People who watch how-to videos tend to have questions about things they aren't sure about, whereas viewers who enjoy videos are more likely to enjoy and share the videos more.

- Subscribers

Another crucial element of engagement that is important to consider is whether users are gaining and losing customers. It is possible to gain an precise understanding of how you can increase your subscribers by filtering the information based on the different types of content, dates and geographic regions.

Chapter 12: Setting your goals

The first thing to do when you decide to start YouTube channels is to determine and define the goals you want to achieve. It is important to understand for why you're doing this and why you're so eager to set up the channel. If you don't have goals and objectives goals, you'll get lost.

This chapter's foundational section is a brainstorming section that will help you contemplate what you would like to accomplish through this channel. In this chapter you will be able to find numerous questions you will need to respond to because it is through these questions that you will get guidance.

What kinds of viewers do you want to meet?

We'll discuss the nature of your channel's demographics in a separate chapter however, prior to that you must be aware about the types of people that will be viewing your channel.

Begin by asking questions such as Do you create content specifically for students at higher education institutions? Are you looking to reach greater female audience rather than males? Are your posts targeted to younger viewers or for an older demographic? What is the geographical region? Do you plan to base your content on specific topics related to a certain area or country? Answer the following questions before you begin!

What is the foundation for your material?

The content on your channel will be what you are offering your audience and you should be aware of the content that it will include at the very beginning. Do you plan to share recipes? Are you planning to participate in reviews of products? Do you like sharing your thoughts on particular areas of human endeavours?

Don't wait until after you've got your equipment or your channel prepared for uploads prior to deciding the type of content. It is advised to take your moment thinking over this concept since it's the content you are going to give viewers and to the YouTube viewers.

Is this venture something that can last?

A few people join YouTube and, at the slightest problem, give up the task because they didn't actually have any long-term strategy at all. If you make a decision and concentrate on a long-term strategy and you are physically and mentally prepared for any challenges that may come your way.

In addition, you'll not put too much pressure on yourself in the beginning, because you know that you've got plenty of time to do things the right way. The long-term plans on YouTube also help you to develop patience on the learning curve. There are many things to learn and you'll have to be patient with yourself.

Are you doing it for leisure or for work?

You must then determine the reason for creating the channel (business or for pleasure). Many people get in the YouTube craze without having a clear idea of what they are looking for which is why they make videos to have fun, and other ones for business purposes, they don't make advancement with either due to lack of determination).

Choose what you would like to achieve even if you're just beginning out because this will help you narrow your goals, assist you to make use of YouTube tools efficiently and allow you to feel fulfilled in this journey.

What other platforms are you planning on connecting to your channel?

Finally, you must be aware of the type of integration plan you are looking for as this will assist you in getting engagement and views. In addition, if you are aware of the integration route you're on early enough and you also focus on the channels you want to use to ensure that you've got a significant following on them.

For instance, if are using Facebook, Twitter, or Instagram and you plan to connect your YouTube channel to these platforms it is now the best time to ensure you have a significant following on these platforms so that you can bring viewers on those platforms on the YouTube channel.

The brainstorming phase isn't an opportunity to think only about the process of setting the channel (this is only a few minutes). Instead, the stage of brainstorming provides a chance to consider ALL things related to the channel, which means once you've started you'll know exactly what you should do and how to start working on it.

However, you must be aware that the majority of the goals and objectives that you come across in the beginning will evolve over time and as you grow as an YouTuber. The YouTube market is an ever-changing one that requires adjustments from the three players that make it work The platform it self, the YouTubers and the users.

If someone is a fan of your channel and your videos doesn't mean they'll remain an avid follower for the rest of time. To keep up with the constant updates on the platform you should examine your goals regularly by using the data of YouTube analytics to figure out the next steps to do.

The objectives you're setting at present are to get going in the right direction However, the goals you'll establish later will help you remain relevant and ensure you're on the right track long-term (or for the duration you wish to stay active on this platform).

Furthermore, having a clear concept of what you want to accomplish as a YouTuber can make it easier to save time because instead of trying to figure out the content you want to film or post, you'll have a plan to follow every single day. Make sure to write down your goals and as you become better you can tweak your goals to produce better quality videos and amazing content.

Now that we've established our priorities now we can get to the actual process that begins with the creation of your own YouTube channel. Follow the next section to learn more about the procedure.

Chapter 13: Create your channel

There is a beginning point for every venture and in this YouTube venture, your first step is to create an account. Once you have established your goals and objectives in beginning this process, you are able to proceed to the next stage by creating the channel. We'll get right onto the next steps

1. Begin by introducing the fundamental ideas

The initial step is to create the channel in just a couple of clicks:

* Signing in to YouTube and then clicking on the user icon located at the top on the display.

After that, click the gear icon. This will bring you to the YouTube settings.

"Click" to "Create an entirely brand new channel."

* Choose "Use the name of a company or other name."

* Enter the name of your brand and click "Create."

You're completed with the first step of opening your channel, however, it's not over.

2. Fill in the "About" section.

Don't forget the "About" section since that is the following step you need to do following the initial step. In this section, you must explain your brand's identity to viewers and explain what they can be expecting from your website. The "About area," you can also include links to other websites as well as social networks. Be concise and imaginative when filling in this section.

3. Channel cover art

Once you've set your channel, you'll be able to see a large banner that shows your channel's name. This banner must be your cover artwork (photo) which presents your channel's name to viewers. You can use YouTube tools that can help you get started with designing your cover artwork; ensure that the image is one that grabs the attention of the viewers and is in line with YouTube's suggested size for photos (2560 by 1440 pixels).

4. Learn about your market and be aware of your content's type

The channel is yours to use however, if you aren't aware of the audience and the audience, you won't know what type of content you should develop. Your content should be targeted towards the particular segment of people you want to attract as viewers. This requires some study. The information you provided and the questions you asked in the first chapter can help you identify the audience to your product.

5. Channel trailer

It is essential to create a channel trailer that is a brief video that introduces your channel to viewers. The trailer informs the viewers about the reason for the channel as well as the type of content they are likely to receive from your channel. Making a trailer is the best method to practice for the main videos that you are going to upload.

6. Create your own video

If you've finished making your first video and now is the time for uploading! But prior to uploading there are actions you must take particularly with regards to editing which will be covered in the following chapters.

7. Optimization process

After uploading the video, you'll need to add the title, tags and description since these are the essential elements that aid in making your video easy to find. Optimizing your video is as SEO on a site and YouTube comes with its own optimization rules that assist you in ranking higher within the YouTube platform. We'll discuss optimization extensively within chapter 7.

8. Consistency

When you launch with your channel on YouTube, don't expect immediate success as it will require time. It is essential to remain constant in your content creation uploads, engagement, and content creation since this will also aid you in staying loyal in this YouTube process.

There are some who think, "I don't have time to record videos and upload each month," well even if you must upload every week, that doesn't mean that you must upload only one video each week. You can set a time set aside to shoot a number of videos and upload each one in succession each week.

9. Integration

Once you've created an online presence, you have to be aware that while YouTube is the YouTube channel is hosted on YouTube but it isn't only available on YouTube. It shouldn't be exclusive to. It is important to transfer your YouTube videos from YouTube to other channels like blogs, social media sites as well as websites.

Integration can help to promote your channel on YouTube. YouTube platform, so that other users are able to access your content. When you are working with your channels, you'll need to increase the number of viewers and subscribers. integration is among the most effective ways to accomplish this.

10. Using engagement

Without constant interactions with your audience there would be no YouTube and that's why you should be prepared for the possibility of participation right from the moment you launch your channel. It is vital to establish a sense of community for your channel, and engage your viewers and ensure that they are at the forefront of your channel.

We will talk about more engagement in chapter 6 and, in that chapter, you'll discover how to create a tight relationship with your viewers, so that each upload becomes an opportunity to make contact with people who gain value from your channel.

11. Channel analytics

We will also be discussing YouTube analysis in a comprehensive chapter, but it is important to be aware that once you have an audience for your channel, it is important to begin looking at your analytics. The analytics can help you optimize your channel to ensure that you can make the best videos in the near future.

By using analysis of your channel, you'll get a better understanding of how people are viewing the videos you have posted, which content they like and how they view. In chapter 5 you will discover the complete guide to how to utilize analytics to get the most performance for your channel.

This chapter gives a brief overview of the steps it takes to set the channel, and an overview of the actions and subsequent steps. There are many more thorough ways to implement some of the concepts and steps mentioned above. We'll be discussing the details in the coming chapters. From this chapter until the final page chapter, we'll take a more in-depth approach to a few of the steps listed above.

In the next chapter in the next chapter, we'll start the process of making the first YouTube video. What are the expectations when you record a YouTube video? Find answers and more information within the following section.

Chapter 14: Filming your videos

After you have created your channel, you must make use of and enhance it by creating and uploading video content, which is the most enjoyable aspect of being YouTuber. Without content and videos your channel will be obsolete, and any other suggestion you'll find in this guide will mean little to your.

But, creating videos shouldn't be considered to be a poor idea , regardless of whether your YouTube channel was intended for entertainment purposes the quality of your video will decide the amount of viewers or subscribers you receive. In this section we will concentrate on the essential steps you should follow to make amazing YouTube videos.

The article will focus on the aspect of pre-creation and the process of creation itself and the editing. The steps listed below are laid out in this sequence; you can follow from the initial step through the last one in a specific order.

The first step is planning!

The first step to create an effective video is preparation. what is the reason you are making the video? Which message would you wish to communicate? The content you create can be informative (if you're teaching something new or an idea) It can be also enthralling (if you're looking to talk about something that can create a discussion).

Your content could be focused on educating (if you intend bring a particular issue to the attention of people and offer solutions). Your strategy should include all the information you require to make the video. This is what you will need to determine your target people, your sales pitch, and any other item you'll need.

These questions will aid you in planning your video prior to filming:

Are my video clips going to contain additional texts or pictures?

* Do I require an script to make this video?

* If I'm going to require an script, what would it include?

In the event that I'm not going to require an script, what kind of audio do I require for the video?

* Can I talk during the recording?

• Will I ever be noticed?

* How do I make the video?

* Where can I film the video?

* Do do I make the edits by myself, or can someone else edit it? (this will let you understand how to handle mistakes)

What type or equipment am I using? right now?

* What is the duration of the video?

* Will I require someone to assist me in recording?

* Do I require an account?

• Who are my intended market?

* What message do I want to convey?

Be sure to take your time in answering these questions as they will assist you to prepare for the creating process.

Step two: Preparing the equipment

After you have your strategy in place now is the time to prepare your equipment and tools. While some tools are static, other equipment is in accordance with the kind of content you are recording. Cameras, microphones, lighting and editors software, memory cards and backdrops are all static therefore they must be set up prior to filming.

Step three: establishing the content stage

With your props and equipment in place, you can make the stage ready and create the area for your recording. In this phase you'll need to find the appropriate background and the best location for your videos. If, for instance, your channel is focused on baking recipes, now is the best time to determine the best location at the table.

If you're recording an unfaced video with no face visible You must set up your content materials and make sure that the location is set for recording. After you've set the stage for your content then take a second glance at the space to make sure that it's correct before beginning recording.

Step four: prepare yourself for taking pictures

A majority of people are preparing to create the video without being prepared for the camera, and when they see cameras, they immediately become anxious, causing their videos full of mistakes. Make sure you are prepared your camera for use by thinking of it as if you were one person with your intended audience. Then converse with this person.

Be aware that you're speaking to someone, not presenting a performance. When you view it as a conversation you'll feel at ease, energized and at ease in the recording process.

Fiveth step: record!

After you've prepared After preparing, it's time to record. that's when your camera turns on, and you begin streaming your video. When recording, keep the camera moving If you do make a mistake while recording, don't stress about it. Just restart the camera and try again without switching off the camera. You can correct everything while editing.

Make sure that you highlight the most important aspects of your content, such as in the case of the product, the focus should be focused on the product. Videos should be entertaining (even even if you're talking about something that is serious) because if you perceive it as a lot of work as well as serious, then it will not be enjoyable for both you and the viewers.

Step six: Editing

After you've recorded your video you must edit the video (because the best work is done by doing more things). This is where you can fix any mistakes you made during recording and make sure your video is ready to upload. When editing, you'll be able to put the scenes in the correct arrangement and cut, and synchronize your sound, and eliminate all footage that is not needed.

By editing you can also include an intro and outro sections, and add additional videos from other sources as well as ensure that your video is in line with the message you wish to convey. For editing your footage, you may require a program with the capability to enhance the video you've made and turn it into an amazing work of work.

There are many editing programs specifically designed for YouTubers that you can employ to help you get your editing correct. When you get access to the program. Don't expect to be pressured to make it perfect the first time. Try it out with random videos before committing to your primary work.

Step seven: Upload your video at the appropriate date and time.

Now that you're finished editing, you are now able to upload your video, however, it should be scheduled at the correct date. For YouTubers it is recommended to have a strategy for uploads, instead of posting on a regular basis. This helps you stay organised and makes it simpler for your viewers and subscribers to know when a new upload is scheduled for them at certain time frames.

Now you've got a better understanding of the best way to create the perfect YouTube channel! Be aware that the fundamental aspect of this process is creating a well-planned plan, first. If you don't have enough planning and you'll have a chaotic procedure. An excellent plan will produce original videos, which will help you create high-quality video content to your YouTube channel.

To make incredible videos, you'll require certain tools and props. We will look at DIY alternatives to use those tools later in our following chapter.

Chapter 15: Simple DIY background ideas for your home.

If someone decides to launch YouTube channels and start a YouTube channel, they are concerned about many things and money is at the forefront of their concerns. However, as a newbie it is not necessary to buy every kind of equipment and tools. You can utilize some basic DIY tips to get started and build upon them as you progress.

When you make your videos, you won't need many props, as the primary elements include a backdrop and lighting, camera, microphone, and all the other items that you'll need to discuss the contents of the video. The props are essential to the video is about for it to be successful. That is to be perceived and heard.

You'll be amazed by the amount of props that you can buy at home and use instead of purchasing them prior to the beginning of your YouTube journey.

Easy DIY Ideas

1. Paper/bedsheet Background

It is necessary to have green screens to shoot your videos to ensure that you don't reveal the backgrounds of the locations you might be during the recording. However, green screens are expensive, and you could replace the green screen with a neat and ironed bed sheet to use as a backdrop. If you don't wish to make use of a bedsheet, you can opt for an art paper in green which is large enough to completely cover the lens that the camera is using.

There's no need to limit yourself to just green background craft paper (this can make your videos repetitive and boring) You can also rotate the colors and add lots of vibrant and vibrant colors like purple, pink, yellow and more.

2. Light

Alongside your green screens, you'll also require studio lighting but these are costly props to get for novices, so what do you substitute instead? To increase brightness, make use of cool-colored, high-lumen lighting bulbs that are not too bright, and also yet not dull.

You can also make use of windows (which is completely free) by filming your videos in close proximity to an open window, which will provide the correct natural light angles for your setup. If you are unable to purchase a professional-grade ring light, you could build your own. With a clear tube of 3ft, LED Strip light and cold show adapter and PVC coupling You can make your own ring light which can help you create well-lit videos.

You don't need to use regular lighting since you can also utilize decorative lights to change the tone for your films. Christmas lights and other festive lighting designs that are a reflection of a specific season (maybe Thanksgiving or Halloween) are fantastic DIY lifting props that you can utilize to add a bit of fun for your films.

3. Sound

Sound is another important element when you create YouTube videos since you need to make sure the viewers can hear your voice. It is also important to ensure that there are no sound echoes or sound waves bouncing off walls. In order to achieve this, you'll need an appropriate sound system and, if you can't buy the most advanced models, you can locate the best microphone to get started.

The best microphones aren't too costly, particularly that are designed for beginners, which is why this is probably one of the items you'll need to purchase. However, having the best mic isn't enough. You must also ensure that there's no other background noise that the microphone can be able to pick up, causing disturbances to the audio.

Make sure you make sure you shoot in a quiet area and, if your windows are open, ensure you have a screenso that you don't get excessive sound from the wind being picked up by the microphone. To reduce echoes it is possible to use an empty plastic container and an item of spandex to create a DIY pop-filter.

4. Visuals: Filming using your smartphone

If you're just starting out or a newbie, you might not have the money to buy an expensive camera or visual kit so why not make use of your smartphone? You can shoot and edit your video with your smartphone. Many smartphones have great cameras that provide amazing photos when you shoot anyplace.

Your phone must be set to selfie mode in order in order to take this picture and you need to find the most attractive camera angle using the selfie mode. Also, do not forget to choose the perfect lighting angle too. This isn't an urgent issue for a beginner but if you could buy a tripod stand then that's great because it can help you keep a steady focus on the subject or object that you are recording.

If you can't afford an excellent tripod stand You can purchase something stable to put your phoneon, and still enjoy excellent angles. Make sure to utilize your rear-facing camera when you wish to have the highest quality video. If you are able to succeed using a smartphone camera, you will be able to succeed using a standard camera when you buy one.

5. Other DIY background ideas

The background itself is crucial, you could make other changes to make it more appealing.

Flower walls are a fantastic option for setting up an online video. they can be created using glue and craft paper. There are plenty of videos that show how to quickly create a flower wall in your home.

In addition, you can apply frames that are engraved with words that correspond to the content of your videos as well as the channel's name in order to provide an even more customized experience.

Flowers from nature are also an excellent idea, especially in the case of an unnatural look to your videos. Sometimes nature could also serve as your backdrop. So why not record videos outside? If you could film your video on the ground, you don't need to worry with props, and you can also create the natural look of your videos.

For a novice it is your responsibility to ensure you are getting the most out of your experience with the least amount of expense starting at the beginning. You are able to always upgrade to more sophisticated equipment and props as you begin developing your channel. We'll move on to the idea that analytics can be used in our following section as we discover how we can make use of the information that comes by YouTube analysis to help make more informed decisions.

Chapter 16: Making use of YouTube analytics to learn how to use it as a beginner

If people hear "Analytics," they hold off from trying to grasp it, because they believe it's a tangled web of numbers and data. However, the reality is that social media analytics aren't nearly as complex as depicted, and it's an essential aspect that every YouTubers must understand (irrespective of whether you use your channel, whether for commercial or leisure).

YouTube analytics can help you comprehend the statistics behind your videos . You can learn about the most watched videos streamed on your YouTube channel. You will also know the people who watch them, and the way the videos are watched. Analytics can also help you understand the most interesting topics which you can replicate in various ways, as these are the topics that draw interest from the viewers.

The user can gain access to YouTube Analytics by simply clicking your logo or avatar that is located next to an upload option. There is a

"Creator Studio" page and that's the location where analytics is (the link to the left).

A brief introduction to YouTube Analytics

The review of YouTube analytics starts with your first login You will be able to see graph pages which give you an understanding of the performance of your channel. You'll also see graphics showing how well you've attracted viewers, the location they are in and how many videos they are watching.

The data you collect through your analysis will appear visually appealing and easy to access Don't take a examine it all in the same way. Make an effort to reduce every data point to the smallest number, and then understand how it can affect your channel's efficiency at a certain level.

Analyzing data

Although the analytics are great to see but you need to understand that it is more than just appearing good. You must look over all your data to improve. If you keep track of your videos every week you'll find some patterns.

You may even find a particular video that has always gained popularity, even though other videos have lower numbers.

You must revisit this particular video to find out the demographics of the people who watch it. Are you getting greater viewers coming that are African countries? If you're advertising to women and gaining greater male audiences, how can you do to turn the flow of viewers?

It is essential to get aware of these statistics since it is by studying them that you'll know how you can improve your website in the near future.

Using demographics

The demographic section informs you who is watching your video and then breaks it down by gender as well as their location and age. For more detailed demographic information it is also possible to determine the exact location and time at which the video was watched.

If you notice that people older than a certain age are more likely to watch your video, then you must make content that meets their needs and their preferences more since they are the ones who can bring in the most viewers.

Verifying the traffic sources

Finding out the source of your traffic from among viewers is vital, particularly in the case of using YouTube for business use. How do people find your videos? What topics or videos receive the most visitors? These questions , along with the data that you gather from the information provided will allow you to identify emerging trends to identify where you can place more focused efforts.

In this section, you'll find individual videos that are sending traffic to your channel and find out how they're arriving at your channel via other websites.

"Device" section "Device" section

The device section will show you the viewers who are watching your videos. Are you using mobile devices? Desktop computers? Laptops? They will also reveal the type of operating system they are using in addition.

Retaining audience

Additionally, there is an "Audience retention" report which will show how many people were watching the entire video or just a small portion of it. It is vital as it allows you to understand the level of engagement the viewers show for your content. Do they find the video relevant enough? Are the videos too long for their tastes? This report also gives the ability to map data-driven locations and dates which can help you narrow your attention on particular regions.

Utilizing engagement reports

Engagement reports are the last choices in your analytics and they provide an in-depth review of the types of videos that users enjoy or dislike. It is also possible to identify those who are subscribed to because of particular videos, and also view the videos that receive the most comments.

In addition, the engagement report can provide insights into the number of engagements that will allow you to understand what prompted viewers to engage in actions. These data can be helpful when curating videos in the future , as you can be able to use them to make more informed and more informed choices.

Do your research and improve

The reason you should look into the analytics is so that you are able to find ways to perform better with your channels particularly if you plan to make it a priority. The data you collect through analytics can aid in advertising campaigns on the internet, and you can use them to increase your visibility and engage.

With the help of analytics, you will be able to spot patterns, trends and swiftly highlight popular topics with your audience and most popular content, leading you to success, as opposed trying to guess which strategies work and which don't work.

Once you begin to maximize the potential of YouTube and begin to understand more about the patterns of your viewers and how you can leverage this to boost engagement. As YouTubers, you should not just look at your videos at the surface, since this could be deceiving and you must go further than that. This is why analytics is crucial.

Chapter 17: How can you keep in touch with the YouTube community?

The idea of analytics that we spoke of in Chapter Five and all the other ideas we've discussed are all based on viewer engagement. Without engagement the social media platforms will be redundant This is especially applies to YouTube.

In conclusion, I would like to be clear that no matter what the goals for setting up the channel, you are responsible for the obligation to ensure that it is active to attract a larger audience and increase your influence through the channel. However If you're already looking to adopt the business model of YouTube the need for engagement should be at a high level because, if there isn't enough engagement your channel will not be visible to your target audience.

Engaging your audience properly isn't about repeating the same thing over and over It's about doing a variety of things simultaneously and with consistency. Your viewers must feel connected to them, and you have to ensure that the time you spend making content is meaningful to anyone.

So , here are some of the best strategies to engage your viewers on YouTube:

Understand your audience

To create a positive engagement it is essential to understand your audience. Who are they? What is their reason for joining? What can you provide them? What are the ways your specialty can help them solve their problems? If you have what the answer to those questions is, you'll be able to figure out how to best engage with the target audience.

Respond to behavior of the viewer in time

Engagement also includes responding to user behavior, but it must be done quickly because this will demonstrate to your viewers that you're dedicated for the greater good of the society. Instead of responding to inquiries two weeks after the date they were posted, attempt to reply earlier than this. Even if you aren't able to respond right away and don't disregard remarks, questions or replies to your questions to respond in a timely manner.

Create a channel and link it to your website.

In order to increase the engagement of your viewers for your channel, you must join your channel on various social platforms to ensure you can reach more viewers for your videos. For instance, if you're using Twitter, Facebook, Instagram or even run a website, make sure to share the links to your videos. You'll be amazed at the number of people who interact with your videos on these platforms.

Interact with your audience

Engaging with your viewers should not be limited to the comment section. In fact, you can engage them when you are filming the video. Instead of speaking all truthfully ask questions and attempt to hear the opinions of your viewers. If you're paying close attention to my writing style you'll be able to spot certain subtile questions I asked and even though I can't listen to your responses these questions will keep your attention in the story.

Make a call to the action

A call to action encourages people to take action when watching your video, or even afterward. An action call could include telling viewers that they should "Like," "Share," "Comment," or any other action that can make the viewer take action which keeps them involved with the video. Be sure to respond to their actions by reading comments and feedback.

Make advice

Sometimes, you need to contact the viewers to find out what they would like you to develop on the channel (remember you're trying to keep good engagement). Ask them to suggest the type of content they would like to read in the comments section. If it's something you're able to make, do it. When you accept suggestions, you're thanking the viewers for their support and making them aware that it's the channel you run, however it's not all about you.

Make use of the playlist

You can also make use of the playlist feature to remain in touch and encourage engagement by connecting your videos and asking viewers to leave feedback about the connection in the content of both videos. For instance, you could upload a video showing how to cook a main dish in two different ways (this is just an example of the food-related niche for vlogging).

The first one, you could invite viewers to click on the link in the description box which takes them to the next method of meal preparation (these videos can be made into an playlist). Ask viewers to comment on the method that works best for them When you do this you'll be generating discussion on your channel as well as seeing views for the videos.

Be aware of your audience as the members of a community

The way you think about your audience determines the way you interact with them. If you think of them as people who just listen to your voice and view your videos, you'll not be able to get the motivation to respond to feedback, and you are always feeling disconnected from the people who watch your videos.

Consider your audience to be an entire community of people who are also committed to the subject you're focusing on via your channel. What are the ways communities can keep their strength? They regularly communicate with each with each other. This is how you boost the amount of engagement you can get in your social media channel.

Engagement is at the core of YouTube because you're making content for a certain segment of people (those interested in your field) and those whom you're creating the content for must to be interested as well. If you do not engage your viewers, you'll be posting videos with no feedback So why would you put in the effort? Following the steps laid out that are in this section, you'll increase your the engagement of your viewers on YouTube.

Have you heard of the phrase "Optimization?" it is one of the most important aspects in developing an effective YouTube channel with a wide reach. Let's find out how to optimize your YouTube channel let's get started.

Chapter 18: Optimizing your channel

Even if you're just starting out it is essential to be focused on optimizing your channel since regardless of the purpose of your channel (pleasure or for business) you'll require viewers to your channel. YouTube channels are now more popular than ever before are now more successful in attracting their viewers' attention. If you are able to enhance your channel, it'll be easy to move from using YouTube for entertainment to turning it a commercial platform.

By optimizing your YouTube channel your company channel will be search-friendly for those who use the app as well as people who use it for regular search queries. Following Google, YouTube is currently the second-largest search engine. Therefore, if you optimize your YouTube channel you'll be able to rank higher.

Before we go into the steps you need to follow to maximize your performance, there are some things to keep in mind that help provide high-ranking signals for optimization and comprise:

Your number of subscriber

YouTube channels that have more subscribers will be ranked higher. Don't be concerned about making this happen since we'll discuss in detail how you can increase your audience and your channel within chapter 9 (if it is your intention to use it for business reasons).

Your user interaction

Do your viewers comment? Like? Share? Subscribe or save?

The duration of your videos.

A majority times, high-quality content also means that the video could be longer in length; this is why videos that run longer than 10 minutes usually rank higher as they provide a wealth of information to viewers.

The video's duration is the time it's watched.

The amount of time it takes for the viewer to view the video and the length of time they remain on the page while they watch the film is an important element.

The top ten methods to optimize your YouTube channel

Post long videos

Long videos are one of the top ranking aspects on YouTube. To get viewers to view the video through from start to finish it is a sign that you are getting more value and the best method to keep them entertained is to make longer-running videos. 10 minutes is a good idea, but make sure to keep it within this limit, so you don't exceed the limit in terms of length.

Include a keyword in the name of your YouTube channel

Make sure that the keywords are integrated into your channel's name in order that when users look up the term, your channel appears. This does not mean that you have to put your keyword for your particular specific niche all over the label, but be imaginative using it in a subtle but deliberate manner.

Update channel trailer

Channel trailers are the same as the graphics of"About Us" and "About us" section. Since they are only accessible to non-subscribers. You must make sure you design an engaging trailer that draws the viewer enough to get them to subscribe.

The trailer you choose to show should contain an introduction to your company, but keep it brief and then ask the viewers to subscribe to your channel as well. Don't directly talk about what you can offer them since they must be on the edge of their seats to discover.

Complete with the "About Us" page.

A lot of YouTubers do not bother with their "About us" page since they don't realize how efficient it can be for SEO. If you're able to fill the page, you'll provide users with a glimpse into the purpose the content of your YouTube channel. This page will help you explain the content of your channel and what kind of content viewers can expect when they sign up. It is important to include on the "About Us" page should also include keywords to help optimize viewers' search.

Strengthen user interaction

The interaction of users is an essential element of optimization. And it's not enough to produce great content. you must also have interaction with viewers. The more people engage with your website or videos the better your ranking chances. Therefore, always share your video or link your videos onto other websites, encourage viewers to sign up, and then reply to your comments (you will be able to learn more about this concept in Chapter Nine when we talk about how to increase the reach of the reach of your YouTube Channel).

Maximize the watch duration (the initial 15 minutes)

In the beginning, if your content don't draw the attention of viewers, then you won't have enough time to watch or viewers who stick with the video until the close. It will be ranked highly enough if you can maximize your the amount of time viewers spend watching by being engaging in your first few minutes.

Use compelling language in your description

Some YouTubers put too excessive emphasis in the video's content their video, but not on their description, which isn't optimal. Make sure to use compelling descriptions as it will result in high rate of click-through. Don't be too long, as it could be dull to read. keep it short enough that each word is meaningful.

Include your keywords in the video

What you put into the video will affect your ranking signals , which is why you should include your keywords in the video, so that it is evident to viewers as well as the search engine. This isn't a reason to be overly enthusiastic about using the word too often. be shrewd and aware of this notion.

Create playlists that can be used to increase the watch time to be set.

Playlists are also an excellent way to increase the time spent on your channel. This is because one playlist on YouTube and then directs viewers to another video, which means that the viewer's attention is diverted between different videos.

If you weave your videos to create an exciting and comprehensive playlist, you'll receive more views for diverse videos. It is also possible to break up long videos down into shorter segments that allow you to let the viewer go to a different journey through different videos. For instance, a one-hour video could be broken into 6 minutes of video and put together into playlists.

Customize thumbnails

Thumbnails make a difference when you have a properly-designed thumbnail, you can create a an unforgettable first impression on your viewers. Your thumbnails need to be distinct from the rest on the page. In order to do this, you need to make use of appealing colors and impressive patterns that match your overall theme. Also, don't over-sell your thumbnails.

Optimizing your channel is an essential move to make however, keep in mind that everything we've talked about so far must be done with a sense of urgency. This is a step-by-step guide to assist you. If you are newbies, I suggest you to take it in a gradual manner. To decide on making use of YouTube seriously for business use You must be aware of its advantages and disadvantages We'll discuss this in the next section.

Chapter 19: The pros and cons of the full-time YouTube job

Everything we've talked about in the past are hints to the fact that you could begin your journey to becoming an YouTuber. The final decision is yours as the notion of becoming an all-time YouTuber has its pros and cons. Before we wrap up this book, we'll need to weigh the pros and cons of each to give you an informed and balanced story that can influence your choice.

The advantages are the benefits of becoming a professional YouTuber

No need for a standard education

You can turn into a full-time YouTuber , without having to go to an institution of higher learning This is one of the most beneficial benefits. All you need to do is begin at the point you're currently in and continue to grow. There are no age limitations either which means you're able to start right today.

You are able to vlog from anywhere

What's more satisfying than being able to work from wherever you're located? Nothing! When you're a full-time blogger you are able to create and upload videos from wherever you are This provides you with a sense of freedom, which allows you to have fun. While you're on holiday, you could film to upload when cooking or caring for your infant, you are able to videoblog, it's an incredible chance to work without a fixed format.

Earn money from the side

A full time YouTuber an excellent opportunity to earn income on the side, or full-time should you choose to make it a priority. You will be doing something that you enjoy, earning money, and remaining current on the internet. If your channel grows to be huge, you'll be earning through multiple channels, including reviews, collaborations, ads trial, unboxing, and so on.

You can do whatever you want to do because you love it

As a YouTuber, you will be able to allow you to do things you love. You get up each day knowing what you can do that makes you feel content. You'll be doing what you enjoy doing if it is also something you love. Consider posting a video on topics that you enjoy with your friends and isn't that a wonderful experience?

You enrich the lives of others

This is an excellent feature and you'll notice it every time you receive a "like" or positive feedback on your blog. Being YouTubers is a certain way to influence others positively and creating value for their lives by sharing your content. People will come up to you and say, "Thank you for sharing the film" and "Well done, you're doing excellently." This is one of the the defining moments that can ensure that you remain determined to keep going.

The downsides that come with being an all-time Youtuber

Consistency

Consistency is a problem for many newbies, and experts are still confronted with this problem. It's easy to explain to the Vlogger "Post every week a video," but when you consider the rigorous editing process and other issues that require consistency, it becomes a major issue. If you're not constant, you won't increase your growth.

Competitiveness

The YouTube market is extremely competitive, even in specific areas so only the most dedicated and talented YouTubers can be able to survive and shine. If a person isn't focused and competitive, he/she might not be constant or be relevant on YouTube.

Breakthroughs can take time

With YouTube you need time and effort to create an audience and gain people to believe in your brand. Even if you follow the correct steps, you'll need to put in a constant effort since the process takes time reach the level you wish to reach. Many people give up after they have tried a couple of times. This can be an issue because even if you return to the same situation over and over, you need to start over.

Production costs for scaling

If you are an aspiring beginner, you might not have many equipment (remember the book that you read about diy props?). It's great as an early stager, but once you're ready to move to become a vlogger you'll have to shell out money on sophisticated equipment. Even although YouTube is completely free when you become more proficient you might need to purchase some things, which can create huge financial pressures.

Trolls or hateful comments

Even if you're doing great and receive praise from your viewers, people may deliberately post negative remarks on your website. The negative comments could be emotionally draining and if you're not mentally prepared these comments will be a burden to you, and stop you from creating content.

Stressful editing processes

Another drawback of being YouTuber is that you're required to undergo a series of stressful editing procedures, which could cause a lot of stress both on time and energy. You'd like to make a videos and then upload them to YouTube, however, you must to edityour video, which is a daunting task, particularly for someone who is new to the field.

In this section you'll have a fair and general concept of what it would be when you become a full-time YouTuber. Each industry that involves social media and use comes with advantages and disadvantages; however, some people are impacted by the negatives more due to the fact that they did not take the time to consider the drawbacks prior to embarking on this YouTube process.

You now know what you'll have to face You also know what you'll be able to do once you start So are you ready to make a decision? Do not rush into the decision now as we have a section to go through that will provide information how beginners can start developing their channel.

Chapter 20: Tips to grow your YouTube Channel

If you've made the decision to accept the YouTube task with seriousness, you'll need to know how to improve your performance as a beginner since the platform is an evolving one that requires creativity to stay in the lead. One indicator that you're making progress on YouTube is when the number of subscribers and reach increase and that is the reason you need to know how to "Grow" your YouTube channel.

When you make the decision to go down this path you should be thinking about the growth potential because it is both an enjoyable and business venture that will produce outcomes. If you aren't ready to take the plunge due to being concerned about the long-term viability of your process, these steps may motivate you to get started.

We'll start by completing an initial step.

Be authentic by using amazing content

There is nothing better than quality content when it comes to growing YouTube channels. It is a concept you must be taking seriously. Make sure your videos have excellent content that inspires viewers to continue watching and share it with others.

Collaboration matters

In order to develop and grow, you must collaborate with others, which is commonplace on YouTube in the present. Although you're a novice it is possible to collaborate with a YouTuber who is the guest or co-host to discuss something related to your area of expertise.

Your collaborator could be someone who has a larger following, which will enable you to reach a larger number of viewers, ultimately increasing the reach of your YouTube channel. Your collaboration may be made into a regular series that takes place during certain times, so that viewers look for the new episode frequently.

Use a single keyword

Making your video around a certain keyword is among the best ways to increase your reach. The keyword should be specific to your niche so that when a user is searching for the exact concept on YouTube your channel will be listed.

Engage your audience

YouTube is a channel for social networking that needs social interaction therefore, you're not permitted to publish videos without engaging with your audience regularly. People want to feel that they're heard and seen even while they interact with you.

Encourage them to leave comments or like, share and sign up. Additionally, engage in a way that you respond to the comments (you are still learning and so comments might not be too difficult for you to manage). Make sure you like the comments and demonstrate you're actively engaged in the channel.